CONTENTS

1)	Introduction to Malcolm Lowry	1
2)	Introduction	60
3)	Style and Method	70
4)	Textual Analysis	
	Chapter I	87
	Chapter II	90
	Chapter III	92
	Chapter IV	94
	Chapter V	96
	Chapter VI	98
	Chapter VII	100
	Chapter VIII	102
	Chapter IX	104
	Chapter X	106
	Chapter XI	108
	Chapter XII	110
5)	Characterization	113

6)	Criticism	135
7)	Essay Questions and Answers	145
8)	Bibliography	153

BRIGHT NOTES

UNDER THE VOLCANO BY MALCOLM LOWRY

Intelligent Education

Nashville, Tennessee

BRIGHT NOTES: Under the Volcano
www.BrightNotes.com

No part of this publication may be used or reproduced in any manner whatsoever without written permission, except in the case of brief quotations in critical articles and reviews. For permissions, contact Influence Publishers http://www.influencepublishers.com.

ISBN: 978-1-645423-14-0 (Paperback)
ISBN: 978-1-645423-16-4 (eBook)

Published in accordance with the U.S. Copyright Office Orphan Works and Mass Digitization report of the register of copyrights, June 2015.

Originally published by Monarch Press.
TK, TK
2019 Edition published by Influence Publishers.

Interior design by Lapiz Digital Services. Cover Design by Thinkpen Designs.

Printed in the United States of America.

Library of Congress Cataloging-in-Publication Data forthcoming.
Names: Intelligent Education
Title: BRIGHT NOTES: Under the Volcano
Subject: STU004000 STUDY AIDS / Book Notes

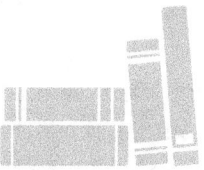

INTRODUCTION TO MALCOLM LOWRY

This Critical Commentary is designed to help you in your study and appreciation of Malcolm Lowry's *Under the Volcano*. But it will make little sense to you unless you are already familiar with the original novel. The author's basic assumption throughout his critical discussion is that it will prompt you repeatedly to refer back to your original text. When he gives you a specific page number (in parentheses), he has in mind the edition frequently used by students: the 1965 edition by J. B. Lippincott Co., Philadelphia and New York. The paperback edition is the Plume Book, New American Library, 1971.

- The Editors

BACKGROUND AND BIOGRAPHY

Early Years. Clarence Malcolm Lowry was born July 28, 1909, to Arthur Osborne and Evelyn Boden Lowry at "Warren Crest," North Drive, Wallasey, England. Wallasey is in Cheshire. It is also near the Mersey River mouth, very near Liverpool, which is in Lancashire County. Confusion concerning Lowry's place of birth arises when one concedes (or doesn't concede) that Wallasey may be a proper part of Liverpool on the Merseyside, and that Lowry may thus be claimed as one of Liverpool's many distinguished native sons (among whom we may include the Beatles). In any event, Wallasey, at the mouth of the Mersey River, contains many docks and possesses the world's largest outdoor swimming pool. The point to remember is that Lowry was exposed to the ocean at a very early age, that he never gave up his extremely mystical faith in the ocean, and that he was enormously impressed with the myriad outdoor pools in Cuernavaca, especially the Olympic-size pool at the Casino de la Selva in that city.

Eridanus, mentioned prominently in *October Ferry to Gabriola* (and in *Under the Volcano*, p. 336) is named after the wreck Eridanus that Lowry saw in Liverpool as a child. Lowry recalled Liverpool, his place of birth, "for I too had been born in that terrible city whose main street is the ocean." Also in *Under the Volcano*, Lowry has Geoffrey Firmin recall his boyhood on the golf links near the Mersey River. It may therefore help to simplify matters to concede that Lowry was born in Liverpool, Lancashire County, England.

In May, 1927, Lowry shipped as a fo'castle hand or cabin boy on a freighter to the Far East. To help him onto that main street of Liverpool which was the ocean, Lowry had himself driven down to the docks in the family Rolls-Royce (his father was a very prosperous cotton broker), a flamboyant gesture that only the Beatles could have appreciated in their latter prosperous days. The berth on the tramp steamer that was to touch Siam, Malaya, the Philippines, Ceylon, the Indian Ocean, and the Suez Canal was secured for Lowry by his father. This was Lowry's idea of the kind of wanderjahre that he wanted to experience before going on to Cambridge University. During the voyage, the sea-struck young man kept a journal which he was later to convert into his first novel, Ultramarine, and which also served as his B. A. thesis at Cambridge.

During his first long vacation at Cambridge, Lowry signed on as a fireman on a Norwegian tramp steamer bound in ballast for Archangel on the White Sea. The ship never got further than Aaleslund in northern Norway, but the voyage did make it possible for him to meet Nordahl Grieg, an author whom he admired tremendously, and to keep a journal which later became the long, unpublished novel, *In Ballast to the White Sea*. On June 7, 1944, the 2,000-page rough manuscript and notes were consumed in the fire that burned down the Lowry's first beach shack in Dollarton, Canada.

Years With Aiken. In 1928 (two years before the Norwegian voyage), Lowry wrote his first letter to Conrad Aiken, an enthusiastic fan letter that he had to write after reading Aiken's novel, *Blue Voyage*. The long "tutorial" and friendship with the older writer is described in greater detail in this Note in the section on Literary Influences. It may be helpful to add at this point that Aiken's autobiographical *Ushant* presents the youthful Lowry as the young alcoholic, Hambo, as "visibly and happily alight with genius." Lowry for his part later referred to the summer of 1929 that he spent with the Aikens at their home in Cambridge, Mass., before he was to enter Cambridge University as the first milestone in his education. He had intentionally gone out of his way on his return from a trip to the West Indies as a passenger in order to get to Boston to meet Aiken. Aiken enthusiastically referred to their vacation together as "that wonderful summer of '29."

Lowry could also thank Aiken for introducing him to Jan Gabrial, an American girl from New York City (and a former "companion" of Aiken's), in Granada in 1933. Lowry subsequently married Jan. She is fictionally present in Aiken's *Ushant* as Nita, Hambo's wife. The portrait of her is very negative. Jan also reminded Lowry of Janet (in *Ultramarine*), and that is probably why he married her. Lowry is also thinly disguised as James Dowd in *I Bring Not Peace*, a 1932 novel by the English writer, Charlotte Haldane. She was not favorably impressed with Lowry.

Travels. Aside from the two "vocational" and one "pleasure" sea-voyages Lowry took, he also spent time in the "fighting of private demons in obscure places," and in less obscure places such as London and Paris, where he found himself literally fighting for mere survival in the early 1930s. In New York City in 1935 he committed himself to the Psychiatric Ward of Bellevue Hospital for a "drying out" period (later described in Lunar Caustic). In 1936, he spent some time in Los Angeles. Later that year, he went to Mexico with Jan Gabrial to begin work on *Under the Volcano*. He also found himself during the years 1936–38 "drying out" in and out of Mexican jails. From May to July of 1937, he was reunited (between stays in jail) with Aiken in Cuernavaca, Mexico. When Jan left him, he returned to Los Angeles in 1938. In 1940, he was divorced from Jan and married Margerie Bonner.

Years In Mexico. Lowry once wrote to a friend that Mexico was "the most Christ-awful place in the world in which to be in any form of distress, a sort of Moloch that feasts on suffering souls." And yet, he (and the Consul) came to Mexico willingly, not impelled by some sense of **epic** or spiritual duty to visit Hell as Leopold Bloom did ("Nighttown" in *Ulysses*); as Dante did ("Inferno" in *The Divine Comedy*); as Virgil had Aeneas do ("Avernus" in *The Aeneid*); or as Homer had Odysseus do ("Hades" in *The Odyssey*). Hell was the abyss splitting the Mexican plateau lying *under the volcano*, the troubled times of the 1930s and 1940s. In *Under the Volcano* the reader may be expected to imagine Christ descending into that abyss for the Easter Saturday Harrowing of Hell. But the Consul is a little less than a self-sacrificing Christ, and it is he, drunk and half-dead, who is hauled by the fascist police into the barranca, the Malebolge, at the end of the novel. For the Consul - and for Lowry - Facilis descensus Averno, "The descent into Hell is easy," as Virgil wrote.

Lowry's actual experiences in Mexico - the loss of his first wife, the drying-out periods in jails, the physical discomforts, etc. - served as a "dry run" (an ironic term to apply to any dipsomaniac) for much of the early plot of *Under the Volcano*.

During their first month in Mexico, Lowry and Jan went by bus to a fiesta in Chapultepec. The bus ride later provides the pattern for the fateful bus ride the Consul, Yvonne, and Hugh take to the Tomalin "fiesta." It is on the fictional bus ride that they see the dying Indian, untouched by human (except for the Pelado's) hands - a symbol of mankind at the mercy of inhuman mankind. The time period covered is 1936–38. During 1945–46, Lowry spent more time in Mexico, this time with his second wife, and it is these "observations" on a Mexico revisited and a Mexico remembered from a previous time that provide the material for *Dark As the Grave Wherein My Friend Is Laid*.

Canada A Potential Paradise. Lowry came to Vancouver, Canada, in 1939 by way of Mexico, Los Angeles, and Hollywood. Soon after, he was joined by Margerie Bonner, who became his second wife in 1940 (December 2), after his divorce from Jan Gabrial. In 1941, he and his wife left Vancouver to settle in Dollarton, where he worked on the final version of *Under the Volcano*. But in 1944, fire - "The Element Follows You Around, Sir!" - burned down their cabin. After a short stay in Niagara-on-the-Lake, Ontario, they returned to Dollarton and built yet another cabin. The nightmare of the fire is fully described (fictionized?) in the posthumously published novel, *October Ferry to Gabriola*. (Lowry's biography is everywhere in his writings!) The winter of 1951–52 may be found carefully recorded (fictionized?) in the novella, "The Forest Path to the Spring." In 1952, the Lowrys decided to escape from under the shadow of eviction, and eventually settled in England in 1954.

In Canada, where Lowry conceived of the great Cordilleras as the "northern cousins" of Popocatepetl, he sought to make of Dollarton a paradise achieved after his "season in hell" under the volcano in Mexico. For this purpose, some aspects of the obviously innocent, innocuous had to be changed, as one would change a stage set in preparation for the next act. Thus, Dollarton is transmuted into Eridanus, a name which represented in mythology both the River of Life and the River of Death. In this way, Dollarton, in actuality a squatters' community threatened with eviction, becomes Eridanus, a community eternally threatened with eviction.

In "The Forest Path to the Spring," an innocent (or at least careless) omission becomes mythologically significant. The narrator can see the oil refinery across the bay from Eridanus. The company sign was eventually to read Shell. So far, the letter S is still missing, and so the sign reads (conveniently for our myth-maker) Hell. The road from hell to paradise must apparently be a two-way street.

The Lowrys were evicted from their beach shack in Dollarton because the authorities wanted the land for a public park. All the beach shacks were burned down. The Lowrys then left for Europe in August, 1954. After a stay in Italy, they went to England, where Malcolm Lowry died on June 27, 1957, in Sussex. At the time, Lowry was waiting for his inheritance, and in the meantime had to live on a remittance of $90.00 a month.

Malcolm Lowry was found dead one morning in June in his cottage in Ripe, Sussex, England, of a combination of drunkenness and an overdose of barbiturates. Someone else explained Lowry's demise as being caused by his choking on his own vomit. In any event, it was a release from a series of chronic illnesses to which he was subjected throughout his life: the Bends, glandular fever, osteomyelitis due to an abscessed tooth, ear infection, possibly T. B., and failing eyesight. He also sustained several near-accidents and operations.

In his own "**epitaph**" prepared for his Selected Poems, Lowry wrote:

"Malcolm Lowry
Late of the Bowery
His prose was flowery
And often glowery
He lived, nightly, and drank, daily,
And died playing the ukulele."

Another "**epitaph**" prepared by a friend of his reads: "Malcolm Lowry: Paradise Regained; Paradise Lost."

Personal Traits. The Yiddish word shlemazl (a person who attracts misfortune) aptly describes Lowry. His whole life was a series of mishaps and near-mishaps, illnesses and ailments of all sorts, attempted suicides, accidents, alcoholism, Delirium Tremens, and fires - fires as man-made conflagrations, fires caused by lightning, fires in volcanoes, fires in alcohol, etc. As the proprietor of the liquor store tells Ethan Llewelyn (Lowry, in *October Ferry*), after the fifth fire in one month has this time burned down Ethan's house, "The Element Follows You Around, Sir!" Indeed, wherever Lowry went, the "volcano" went with him, even in that "Northern Paradise," Canada.

Unlike Faulkner, who used drinking as a stimulus (sic) to sustained writing, Lowry used sustained writing as an antidote or preventative to drinking. On dry, sober days, Lowry wrote from twelve to sixteen hours a day. He took almost six years to rewrite several chapters of *Under the Volcano*, sometimes keeping as many as twenty versions of a single paragraph going at the same time. This, not necessarily because he was trying to emulate Flaubert's le mot juste - although he was a genuine precisionist, and at times as fussy as Henry James (but see Lowry's frequent non-Flaubertian, Jamesian long, involved sentences) - but because sustained writing kept him away from drinking.

It can be said of Lowry, as of the Consul, that "his cosmos was all ego." Lowry refused to be excluded from his fictions. They were not intended to be "escapes from personality" in the T. S. Eliot sense. Almost every substantive situation in *Under the Volcano* (and his other works) reflects to a considerable degree many situations which he himself had experienced at one time or another. Lowry distributed his own personality among several of his characters.

Through his own writing Lowry obviously pursued his own identity through the "labyrinth of his experiences." There is something so legendary, even mythic, about his own life (Childe Malcolm's Pilgrimage) that one finds it almost impossible to separate the experiences of his own life from those of his fictional heroes. It is as if Lowry had come upon some sort of fantastic time machine through which he was able to write the scenario of his life after he had lived it.

Lowry was not a regional writer (despite what latter-day Canadian critics say). He was at home and not at home in Canada, Mexico, Europe, or anywhere else. Like Coleridge's Ancient Mariner, he was doomed to retell his cosmic, never-ending voyage. The intention is aptly implied in the title that he himself had chosen for his all-inclusive, massive work: *The Voyage That Never Ends.*

Lowry's Philosophy. The Canadian critic Bradbrook says that "...the strength of Lowry's work lies in its negation of advocacy or didacticism." His artistic imagination was strongly rooted in nomadism and internationalism. He anticipated the more modern existentialists in recognizing at an early time the absurdity of modern existence, the feeble ways available to meet death heroically. The Consul is a universal rather than a particularized figure. Consequently, Lowry himself emerges as a general, rather than a personal, advocate. Apart from the Consul's (and Lowry's) chronic drunkenness, he was still qualified to ask: How can we avoid the descent into Hell? How can we extricate ourselves from Hell? Says the Consul: "There is no explanation of my life." The Consul can only carry on his "battle for the human consciousness."

Lowry (and Geoffrey Firmin) hoped to elude (or transcend) the specter of death by magic - the magic of alcohol, the magic of Cabbalism and other forms of numerology (especially the numbers 7 and 12), and the magic of words (Why else do we "spell" words?), the latter most appropriate for a writer, one who can cast "spells" with words.

Lowry was a neo-Buddhist of sorts (as we shall try to prove later); one need but consider the constant references to the Buddhistic "Wheel of Eternity."

"The image of the dying voluptuary sums" up nature as well as man," says Eleanor Widmer, "and Malcolm Lowry as well as the Consul."

Lowry saw modern man as fragmented, besieged by multiple desires, prevented by fate or bad luck or whatever one chooses to call it, from achieving wholeness. For the Consul - and for Lowry - it was virtually an extraordinary achievement to have become merely a "divided" man. In short, Lowry may have sincerely recommended that we accept the "schizophrenia" of modern man as "normal."

CHRONOLOGY

1909 (Clarence) Malcolm Lowry born July 28 at "Warren Crest," North Drive, Wallasey (Merseyside, Liverpool), England, to Arthur Osborne Lowry, prosperous cotton broker and strict Methodist, and Evelyn Boden Lowry (presumably of partial Norwegian descent).

1919–1926 Operated on several times for chronic eye disorder; attended Leys School, Cambridge.

1927 Embarked on first sea-voyage in May as cabin boy and reached the Far East, Southeast Asia, and eventually the Suez Canal. Diary notes later converted into first novel, *Ultramarine*.

1928 After reading Conrad Aiken's novel, *Blue Voyage*, wrote first of several letters to that author.

1929 Spent first part of the summer as passenger on a ship to the West Indies; latter part, with Aiken at Cambridge, Mass.

1930 In summer, shipped out on a Norwegian freighter as fireman; when trip was abruptly curtailed, succeeded in meeting Nordahl Grieg, Norwegian poet and novelist;

Grieg possibly prototype of Lowry's most common persona, Sigbjorn Wilderness.

1932 Graduated from Cambridge University with third-class honors in the English tripos; received B. A. degree; graduation thesis the novel *Ultramarine*; went to France.

1933 *Ultramarine* published by Jonathan Cape in London. Spent the summer in Granada, Spain, with the Aikens; met Jan Gabrial there, married her in December.

1933–1934 First American publication of his works, short stories, in Story magazine, edited by Whit Burnett and Martha Foley.

1935 Brief period in New York City alone; self-committed to Bellevue Hospital for "drying-out" session; "fictionized" in *Lunar Caustic*.

1936 Went to Los Angeles; joined his friend John Davenport in Hollywood worked on several film scripts, including F. Scott Fitzgerald's *Tender Is the Night* (never used). In November, went to Mexico with first wife, Jan; began work on *Under the Volcano*.

1937 Reunion with Conrad Aiken in Cuernavaca, Mexico, during period of May to July; Jan separates herself from Lowry.

1938 Back to Los Angeles. Critical Battle of the Ebro in the Spanish Civil War. Met Margerie Bonner in Hollywood.

1939 Went to Vancouver, British Columbia (Canada) in July of that year.

1940 Divorced from Jan Gabrial; married Margerie Bonner in December. Settled down in beach shack in Dollarton (near Vancouver) as a "squatter."

1941 Met Charles Robert Stansfeld Jones, a census enumerator in Dollarton, and came to know the Cabbala through him; Jones also known as "Frater Achad." After third version of *Under the Volcano* was rejected by twelve publishers, manuscript was withdrawn from agent, and fourth and final version of novel begun.

1944 June 7, Dollarton shack burned down; went to stay with Cambridge classmate, Gerald Noxon, in Ontario. Final, acceptable version of *Under the Volcano* completed on Christmas Eve.

1945 Returned to Dollarton in February, began to rebuild house. In the fall, went to Mexico with Margerie; that experience "reported" in *Dark As the Grave Wherein My Friend Is Laid*.

1946 Final corrections, revisions, and "defense" of *Under the Volcano* made (see letter to Jonathan Cape, January 2, 1946). Fourth and final version of novel accepted for publication simultaneously by Cape in London and Reynal and Hitchcock in New York. In May, following acceptance of novel, returned to Dollarton with Margerie. In December, sailed with wife on freighter to Haiti.

1947 Went to New York in February for publication of *Under the Volcano*; returned to Dollarton; in November sailed to France on a French freighter; the passage through the Panama Canal on that trip later became the short story "Through the Panama."

1949 The return to Dollarton, writing and collation of the stories to be posthumously published as Hear Us O Lord from Heaven Thy Dwelling Place.

1950–1954 Intensive period of work on four novels, short stories, poems.

1954–1955 August in New York, final reunion with Aiken, sailed 1955 on an Italian freighter for Genoa with wife; spent winter in Taormina, Italy.

1955 Final move, this time to Ripe, in Sussex, England.

1957 Died not unexpectedly on June 27 of lingering addiction to alcohol and barbiturates. Had almost completed final novel, *October Ferry to Gabriola*.

1961 Beginning of posthumous publication of all works except *Ultramarine* and *Under the Volcano*. Hear Us O Lord from Heaven Thy Dwelling Place published.

1962 A revised version of *Ultramarine* first published in U.S. Selected Poems published.

1963–1964 In winter, publication of typescript of germinal short-story version of *Under the Volcano* in special Lowry issue of Prairie Schooner magazine in Canada.

1965 First hardcover reissue of *Under the Volcano* in December; also of Selected Letters, edited by Margerie Bonner Lowry and Harvey Breit.

1968 Publication in summer of *Dark As the Grave Wherein My Friend Is Laid*; in the fall, Lunar Caustic in England; in winter, screen rights to *Under the Volcano* sold.

1970 Publication of last novel, *October Ferry to Gabriola*, in the fall.

1973 Official biography by Douglas Day published by Oxford University Press.

LOWRY'S THEMES, MOTIFS, AND TECHNIQUES

To sense the nature and character of the man who wrote *Under the Volcano*, one has but to examine the three epigraphs that introduce the novel. From Sophocles' affirmative statement of faith in humankind, to Bunyan's negative cry of despair, to Goethe's reaffirmation of faith and confidence in mankind, one can trace the vacillation, the doubt, the black despair that engulfed this man throughout his life.

"Wonders are many, and none is more wonderful than man," Sophocles exclaims. Here is the upbeat faith in mankind that might have saved Lowry from the depths of the abyss, the real and the imagined one. "Yea, he hath resources for all; without resource he meets nothing that must come," Sophocles affirms and reaffirms. "Only against Death shall he call for aid in vain; but from baffling maladies he hath devised escapes."

Had Lowry subscribed to Sophocles alone, he might have been saved from the early abyss that claimed him as unmistakably as it claimed the Consul. But he chose to seek out the advice of John Bunyan, as well as Sophocles. What did he find in that seventeenth-century pessimist? "Now I blessed the condition of the dog and toad, yea, gladly would I have been in the condition of the dog or horse, for I knew they had no soul to perish under the everlasting weight of Hell or Sin, as mine was like to do." Is this Lowry's latent Calvinistic Methodism at work?

The **allusion** to Bunyan is the unmistakable setting for the cry of despair annunciated by the Consul: "Yet that which added to my sorrow was, that I could not find with all my soul that I did desire deliverance." This Was The Consul, Rejecting Deliverance In The Best Manner Of The Calvinist Literalist Accepting His Pre-destined Fate.

The quotation from Goethe affords the Consul (and Lowry) one more chance, one more affirmation of faith in mankind: "Whosoever unceasingly strives upward...him can we save." One cannot be saved, unless one wills to be saved. The Consul did not will to be saved. Nor did Lowry wish to be saved from the black abyss of eviction, dispossession, alienation, that he cultivated as a latter-day "ancient mariner" destined to repeat, albeit figuratively most of the time, the eternal voyage and the recounting thereof.

Major Themes. Le Gusta Este Jardin?... Evite Que Sus Hijos Lo Destruyan! "Do you like this garden?... Those who destroy it are evicted!" Firmin more or less translates the message written on a wall. The garden is literally the one which Firmin's wife had carefully-and hopelessly-cultivated, and which the Consul had allowed to be overgrown during her absence. The garden is also the rich, lush garden that is Mexico, prodigiously endowed by nature, now spoiled (and despoiled) by its neo-fascist politics (cf. Firmin's eventual assassination by the fascist police). It may also symbolize the promising garden of the world, contaminated by World War II.

Social man was once primitive, natural, innocent man. Before society began to encroach upon the "wilderness," the natural man existed in every human being. But now, this confused and fragmented social man, all that is natural smothered within him, is alienated from his own consciousness and from the world of nature. The fundamental conflict that arises from this condition is that between social man's attempt at a logical and rational view of existence and primitive man's unquestioning acceptance of all life.

Like Faulkner's attitude toward the Indians of his South, his primitives, Lowry found a similar innocence in the Mexican Indians. Social man can find no satisfying answers to his cosmic questions about life and death, and is therefore disabled by increasing disillusionment, and finally falls into black despair. Primitive, natural man, on the other hand, finds no need to explain or interpret life or death (cf. the way in which the Mexican natives celebrate the Day of the Dead. More on this below). Through his unquestioning acceptance of these two basic phenomena in nature, he is able to achieve an enviable peace of mind and real strength with which to cope with the struggle for existence.

The garden in the final analysis is the Biblical Garden of Eden from which Adam was evicted for asking questions inconsistent with his blessed state of innocence. Perhaps this is what Candide also meant when he advised (or was advised) to cultivate one's garden. Lowry himself wrote, in connection with October Ferry to Gabriola, that the book dealt with "the **theme** of eviction, which is related to man's dispossession, but this theme is universalized..."

Widmer speaks of "the tenuous exaltation of man, cast from paradise into a harsh, alien, fragmented world that betrays him with unfulfilled promises." Though the book is about a self-destructive alcoholic living in an admittedly violent environment, "its infernal thrust extends beyond the confines." The abandoned man, as Lowry readily recognized, "could find hell everywhere in an irreligious world."

The correct translation of the whole garden motto quoted earlier is: "Do you enjoy this garden/Which is yours?/Keep your children from destroying it." It is simply and innocently the equivalent of a "Keep Off The Grass" sign. The Consul mistranslates it; there is absolutely nothing about "eviction" in it. Evite is the imperative form of the Spanish verb evitar, meaning "to avoid or shun." The Spanish verb for "evict" is expulsar or desalojar. The Consul's sense of guilt causes him to mistranslate miserably (he knew Spanish rather well), anticipating his imminent doom.

No Se Puede Vivir Sin Amar. "It is not possible to live without love," reads another sign on a whitewashed wall. This second key motto annunciates yet another major **theme** of the novel. How can evicted, dispossessed, alienated man achieve grace? the Consul keeps asking himself throughout his journey (as Lowry kept asking himself throughout his many journeys and voyages on land and sea, driven like the Wandering Jew [cf. Chapter 20, *October Ferry to Gabriola*] from one country to another, from one home to another). In the end, Firmin discovers that the inability to love is the greatest sin of all against mankind. Had he truly loved Yvonne, had he loved Hugh, it might have been they, rather than his enemies, who would have taken possession of his wounded body. Because he failed to reciprocate the love that Yvonne and Hugh gave so willingly to him, he paid with his life: his enemies cast him into the barranca, to die like a dog.

The Consul suffered from acedia, Stephen Spender observes, the spiritual apathy that causes men to refuse to love or be loved. Firmin is compelled to reject love in order to be alone; in the end, he has to be killed because he rejects love. He is fully aware of this fact, but he is incapable of doing anything about it. And so he drinks in order to live with this dilemma.

The Consul, then, is painfully aware of what is more than a personal dilemma. The world, as he sees it, is suffering from its inability to love or be loved. He is a modern hero, a tragic hero - even an anti-hero - who is charged with reflecting the "extreme external situation within his own extremity." And, with no pretensions of Christliness (Spender believes), he will die to show the world what it means not to love or be loved. For his part, Lowry quite early became the prototype of those artists who, despite inordinate self-involvement, alcoholism, and narcissism, could be lucid though drunk, and in their very supernormal excesses seem to attain a quality of saintliness - not martyrdom, not self-pity - as though enduring, what in laymen and non-artists might appear to be sins, transgressions, or vices, for the sake of all of us. In short, Lowry may have been one of the first to exemplify the "artist as messiah."

Good Samaritan. A logical corollary to the "life without love" **theme** is the guilt motif as expressed through the parable of the Good Samaritan (Luke 10:3–37). The key chapter of the novel, Chapter VIII, tells the story of the Indian dying on the roadside, with nobody daring (or willing) to help him. The chapter, originally presented as a short story, is based on an actual experience by Lowry and his first wife, Jan, on a trip through Mexico. The **episode** remained permanently fixed in Lowry's mind. Over the years, it assumed more cosmic, universal connotations: man's refusal to assume responsibility for his brother's welfare; man's inhumanity to man; man's increasing indifference or cruelty toward his fellow man. The sense of guilt became so particular, so personal, in the Consul's case, that he felt need to atone for such guilt, and the eventual refusal to accept any of the help proffered him, one must conclude, led him to his predictable self-destruction. No se puede vivir sin amar.

Sobria Inebriata. Philo, a later Roman writer, coined the phrase sobria inebriata, an oxymoron which translates literally as "sober drunknenness"; in a more figurative sense, the phrase means a special kind of drunkenness brought on by drinking but resulting in a state of sobriety bordering on "translucent clairvoyance."

The Consul is a lonely drinker; not lonely because he drinks or wants to drink by himself, but a drinker because he is lonely, or alienated. In his pathetically helpless way, he has been reaching out for companionship since his boyhood days (according to Laruelle). He may also drink because of his fear of sex (and/or love), his rejection of a world with failed values, his deeply ingrained puritanism (Firmin is said to have attended a strict Wesleyan school), and (possibly) suppressed homosexual tendencies.

Like other heavy drinkers, Firmin has the capacity to drink himself into a state of drunkenness bordering on "translucent clairvoyance." He believes he can reach his fullest consciousness only through drinking mescal, a belief, incidentally, shared by many Mexican Indians. They will use mescal or any other liquor derived from peyote or maguey to put themselves into the proper state of clairvoyant consciousness to accept religious revelations. So Firmin experiences a kind of Black Mass through mescal. As Lowry himself pointed out, similar states of consciousness cannot be achieved through excessive imbibing of beer, wine, or any other of the Anglo's spirituous liquors.

Mescal is a liquor made from the leaves, juicy stalk, and roots of certain species of maguey (see also amaryllis below). It is also made from pulque, the fermented sap of the agave plant. Tequila and sotol are similar to mescal. Then there is mescalin, an alkaloid drug obtained from peyote, with a psychedelic, hallucinogenic effect similar to that obtained from mescal.

The Mexican amaryllis is a non-bulbous species of the agave plant. The snowdrop species of amaryllis, naturalized and cultivated in Europe and in the Western Hemisphere, has a flower symbolic of consolation and of promise. And similar to this is the tuberose, a waxy-flowered plant. The amaryllis thus becomes a fairly important symbol in the novel itself.

Firmin probably uses mescal, which is similar in effect to mescalin, as the Mexican Indians (and some New Mexican Indians) use mescalin as a mind-expander, preparatory to experiencing some kind of "epiphany" (cf. the "bathroom epiphanies" throughout the novel, especially in the very late pages).

The juice of the maguey plant (pulque) was first called "honey water" by the Toltecs of Mexico. The Aztecs adopted this "honey-water" and made pulque a sacred potion. They considered it particularly holy for the god of fire (cf. whisky, literally "water of life"; compare this with the Scandinavian aquavit, aqua vitae, i.e., "water of life"), possibly because it gave them such a warm feeling inside (cf. slang term for whisky, "fire water"). Eventually the plant itself was deified. It was represented by a separate goddess, who had 400 rabbit sons (cf. later, rabbit as Aztec symbol for drunkenness. The rabbit also appears in Aztec hieroglyphic writing to express the various degrees of drunkenness. The number of rabbits shown indicated how much a man was "under the influence").

Alcoholism is but one factor in the destruction of Geoffrey Firmin. He is in fact immobilized (with or without the help of alcohol), full of fear and doubt, a stranger whose alienation is reinforced by the exotic nature of the place in which he lives. Lowry himself feared that the nearly simultaneous publication of his novel with Charles Jackson's *The Lost Weekend* (popular saga of yet another alcoholic) would cause readers to overemphasize Firmin's alcoholism, to the detriment of the other facets of his very complex character. The Consul's drinking (he is drunk for about three-fourths of the novel) is not to be construed as symptomatic of ordinary drunkenness. True, he feels guilty about being constantly borracho, but it is this same drunkenness that "frees his language so that it approaches poetry. In the same way, madness evoked poetry in Lear, chivalry did the same for Cervantes (in *Don Quixote*)." Firmin can't wait until the cantinas open in the morning. The cantinas (cf. song?) are named for their music as well as for their mescal. The Consul will enter one soon "to fashion a song from the rhythms of alcohol" (Gass). When Firmin makes inadequate love to his wife, it is as if he were playing upon his wife's body, he performing, she the instrument. Love for him thus becomes a kind of alcohol-sponsored music-making.

"Fundamentally," writes Stephen Spender, "*Under the Volcano* is no more about drinking than King Lear is about senility... Just as the collapse of power in King Lear is envisioned through the shattered mind of the king, so in *Under the Volcano* is the tragic despair of Mexico, and, beyond Mexico, the hopelessness of Europe torn by the Spanish Civil War, seen magnified and distorted in the minds of the Consul and of Hugh." Along with *Ulysses* and *The Waste Land, Under the Volcano* must be understood as a book about the breakdown of values in the 1920s and 1930s.

Cabbalism A Major **Theme**. In 1941, census enumerator Charles Robert Stansfeld Jones called at the Lowry cabin in Dollarton in his official capacity. In the course of their conversation, Lowry learned that Jones, a former portrait painter, was known to be an authority on the Cabbala - he was "professionally" known as "Frater Achad" - and had written extensively on the subject. Other conversations followed Lowry's decision to become a pupil of Jones, and Lowry eventually found in Jones' books (especially in Q. B. L. with its diagram of the Tree of Life) a framework in which he could systematize some of his vague concepts about fate, coincidence, chance, and the like. Much of what Lowry learned from Jones (in particular about the *Zohar*, the key book of the Cabbala, which Lowry never read but relied on Jones' interpretation of it) duplicated Lowry's own independent reading in mysticism and hermeticism before 1941. What Jones can do for the reader of *Under the Volcano* is to provide him with a key after the fact to a large number of the Cabbalistic symbols in the novel.

The Cabbala was used by Lowry in a metaphorical way because it represented man's spiritual aspiration. The Etz Chaim, or Tree of Life, which is its emblem, is described by Lowry as "a kind of complicated ladder with Kether, or Light, at the top and an extremely unpleasant abyss some way above the middle..." For the Consul, however, who had been a Cabbalist and was familiar with the Cabbala's mystical tenet that the abuse of wine (or any other alcoholic beverage) is associated with the abuse of mystical powers, his spiritual domain was more likely the Qliphoth, the world of spells and demons, symbolized by the Tree of Life upside down.

All this having been said (by Jones and by Lowry), Lowry himself cautioned the reader that "all this is not important at all to the understanding of the book"; that it was only one approach to the book, albeit a fascinating one. "I just mention it in passing," Lowry insisted, "to hint that, as Henry James says, 'There are depths.'" Nonetheless, as late as 1950 Lowry was convinced that he had intended to portray the Consul as a kind of black magician, that is, a man who has all the elements opposing him. He had written (or rewritten) Chapter X in 1942 (he had been studying with Jones for a year by then), and it is in that chapter that the Consul himself enumerates all the elements (actually, the chemical elements) that are against him. The implication is (according to Lowry) that "an analogy is drawn between Man today on this planet and a black magician."

Lowry was a Cabbalist; but only in the same sense that he was a jazz buff, an aficionado of Elizabethan poetry (especially Marlowe's), a golf enthusiast, an amateur psychologist, a seafarer. Above all, he was a highly cultured man, a widely-read writer who seized upon anything and everything to help him plumb the depths of the human psyche. What influenced him most, a Canadian critic has said, "was really life itself, with its complexity, its fatefulness, its coincidences, and its hidden potential." It is significant to note that when Lowry did get to Canada, he was finally able to sort out much of the shreds and patches of information he had accumulated during his many years of wandering and wondering. The Cabbala, then, provides but one of several "glosses" for his peculiar, idiosyncratic writings.

"The infinite complexities of cabbalistic ritual are enacted symbolically and consciously in the Consul's daylong progress toward death," explains Warren Dodson, "whereas Stephen Daedalus and Mr. Bloom quite unconsciously perform mythic mimicry." Lowry's "superficial" use of the Cabbala (probably because of his overambitious intention to create a Faustian character in the Consul) points up the Consul's inferiority to Stephen and to Bloom. The Consul is intended to be Everyman, but his idiosyncratic shortcomings and frequently unconvincing intellectuality make him somewhat unacceptable in that role. He lacks the universality of Stephen (and Stephen's intellectuality) and of Bloom (and Bloom's compassion and humanity).

Theme Of Duality. Lowry himself suggested that the structure of his novel resembled a Churrigueresque Mexican cathedral, with Chapter I as the westerly tower and Chapter XII as the easterly tower. This is but one of several dual symbols that may be found throughout the book, suggesting a **theme** of duality intrinsic to the novel. Other twin symbols might include:

1. The twin volcanoes, Popocatepetl ("the smoking mountain") and Ixtacihuatl ("the sleeping lady"). The Consul is Popocatepetl (the Mexicans call this volcano "He"); Yvonne is Ixtacihuatl (the Mexicans call this volcano "She"). "He" is smoking, but extinct; "She" is "sleeping," unaroused by the impotent "He." The love that could never be consummated!

2. The twin towers or miradors in front of Jacques' house (Chapter VII). One tower is ornamented with angels and cannonballs, and may be said to represent the Consul and the conflict within him between good and evil. The other tower is unadorned, simple, and may be said to represent Yvonne. The towers are described by Lowry as "tiny roofless variants of the observation posts which everywhere commanded the valley in Quauhnauhauc," the "valley of the shadow of death" (Lowry's tentative title for *Under the Volcano*). From his own twin "observation posts," Laruelle is able to oversee the central tragedy of the novel.

3. The more general antitheses, paradoxes, and ambiguities, such as the prophecy of doom vs. the plea for love, the tormented alcoholic vision vs. the sober statement of faith, the past vs. the present, despair vs. hope; and, more particularly.

4. In Chapter I, the scene at the Cafe de la Selva (selva = woods) refers to Dante's Inferno as well as to the woods where Yvonne is murdered.

5. The time of the novel: The Day of the Dead. The local cinema is showing Las Manos de Orlac, the same film shown exactly one year ago on the day of Firmin's death.

6. The picture of the man in the film with bloody hands symbolizes mankind's guilt, the Consul's guilt; also the guilt of Firmin's double, Laruelle, the failed moviemaker.

7. Same picture: symbolizes the blood of the murdered Indian; also the blood on the hands of the pelado, or thief.

8. The drunken horseman (Death, one of the Four Horsemen of the Apocalypse?) seen by Laruelle, may also symbolize Firmin, and/or mankind. (The horseman image likewise adumbrates the murder of both the Indian and Yvonne.)

9. The Ferris wheel in the square that Laruelle observes is turning backward: it may symbolize the Buddha's wheel of eternity. On the other hand, since it is being observed - and interpreted - by a film-oriented man, it may also symbolize the flashback itself (the essential drive of the novel), the wheel (or reel) of film (or journey) reversed. This ties in neatly with Lowry's earlier "throwaway" symbol of the film Las Manos de Orlac, which may (a) have been playing for one full year from Nov. 2, 1938, to Nov. 2, 1939 (stop-action of film on projector), or (b) is playing again one year later (reverse action of film on projector).

Day Of The Dead Motif. Why did Lowry decide on Mexico as the locale for the novel? Some reasons have already been given, others will be suggested later. There are also very cogent reasons why he chose November 2, the Day of the Dead, for the time frame of the novel. The obvious reason is that this novel is death-oriented. A secondary reason is that Mexico, the locale of the novel, is death-oriented, that on November 2, the Mexicans, a peculiar mixture of pagan, primitive peoples and a super-imposed (but only partially assimilated after almost 400 years) European, Christian culture, look upon that day as a happy, annual time of reunion with the spirits of the departed. This is in itself not so unique; many lands, many cultures, many religions annually commemorate the departure of their kinfolk from this life. But in Mexico, long before November 2, death manifests itself in some of the most unusual forms: in the windows of pastry shops by the skulls of dough or confectionary sugar that lovers present to each other; in the toys of children in the form of miniature: coffins with skeletons inside; in other small caskets containing dead babies made of sugar; in tiepins in the form of skeletons.

During this sacred (or macabre) period, street vendors hawk poems mocking both the dead and the living. More seriously and soberly, the Day of the Dead is the occasion for visiting graves. At home, incense and candles are burned in honor of the dead. And in the public squares, the air of carnival is all-pervasive. And the Ferris wheel!

Theme Of Buddhism. The Ferris wheel of the Day of the Dead festival may be compared with the burning wheel of Buddhist law, "its steel twigs caught in the emerald pathos of the trees" (Gass). The wheel as symbol recurs as often as the author's design requires.

Lowry himself endorses this interpretation of the Ferris wheel. The Consul was born in the Himalayan region of India, and is no stranger to Zen Buddhism. It is therefore safe to assume that the Consul was familiar with the Buddhist wheel of the law, the wheel of eternity; that he was also familiar with the "Sermon of the Turning of the Wheel of the Law" as delivered by the Buddha at the deer park at Sarnath, from which we quote briefly:

A. The "Four Noble Truths"

1. Existence is sorrow

2. Origin of sorrow is desire

3. Sorrow ceases when desire ceases

4. Way to achieve cessation of desire is the "noble eightfold path"

B. The "Noble Eightfold Path"

1. Right belief

2. Right resolve (to renounce sensual pleasure, to harm no living creature, and ultimately to attain salvation)

3. Right speech

4. Right conduct

5. Right occupation

6. Right effort (to keep the mind free from evil and devoted to good)

7. Right contemplation

8. Right meditation (to achieve a state of selfless contemplation)

Then there is also Buddha's Fire Sermon against the fires of lust and other passions. Between the Buddha and the Cabbala, how could the Consul have gone so wring? The Buddhists Also Take A Strong Vow Against Strong Drink! Nevertheless, Lowry for his own part does try to reconcile or synthesize Buddhism and other Eastern religions with Christianity (cf. pp. 307-8).

Fire And Water Motif. "The archetypal and mutually compensatory themes of fire and water [run] throughout Lowry's life and work," says Richard Costa. The Consul always wished for a water-wreathed Northern Paradise; instead, he fell to his death "through the blazing of ten million burning bodies" under the volcano. Thoughts or visions of fire always evoke for the Consul corresponding visions or images of water. Water images predominate in Chapter V - lake, waterfalls, rain - suggestive of regeneration (the garden's obvious "thirst"), the "certainty of brightness." Tequila and mescal represent for the Consul a kind of "holy water," a means to achieving greater consciousness, awareness, even a clairvoyance. "I have to have a drink or two now, myself..." he tells Laruelle, "else I shall become confused, like yourself." But his final contact with "water" is "the noise of foisting lava in his ears," as he is carried to the edge of the barranca, to his death. The regenerative water, the mysterious river Eridanus that can put out the flames and cool the body (as it cooled the body of the mythical Phaethon), is never reached.

In Section Four of Eliot's *The Waste Land*, "Death by Water" is a description of the happier fate of a drowned Phoenician sailor, who (with delicious **irony**) at least is not dying (like us moderns) of thirst in a parched wasteland. His death by drowning promises no resurrection, but at the same time there is a strange, strong sense of peace in his death. The Consul would have envied him such an end. The Consul always hoped that he might eventually transcend the ashes of his fiery life. There was always the hope of some magical, regenerative "water" that would quench the fire. In his wildest visions, perhaps under the influence of mescal, he might have envisioned a submarine volcano, a symbol of the best of two possible worlds, of self-indulgence with instant forgiveness and redemption at hand.

"The only hope, or else despair/Lies in the choice of pyre or pyre - /To be redeemed from fire by fire" (T. S. Eliot, "Little Gidding" in *Four Quartets*). For Lowry it was always fire and water (another example of the duality that pervades his works): fire as in *Under the Volcano* and in the many fires in *October Ferry to Gabriola*; water as in the several sea voyages Lowry took, and in drink. Lowry eventually "drowned" when he choked to death in his own vomit during a drunken stupor. "We only live, only suspire/Consumed by either fire or fire" (Eliot).

Volcano As **Theme**. Lowry's Mexico is a southern hell, an Inferno (the smoking volcano). The volcano is not one volcano but many, the names of which (as indicated earlier) immediately become symbolic. The archetypal volcano is at once infernal and redemptive. The path along the side of the volcano is both an ascent and a descent. In Yvonne's death vision (Chapter XI), it is an ascent from fire to light; in the Consul's death vision, it is a descent from light to fire.

Spanish Civil War As Motif. The Consul has his Good Samaritan fixation about the Indian dying on the roadside; Hugh has his Good Samaritan fixation about the Loyalists losing in the Spanish

Civil War. Through his half-brother Hugh, the Consul likewise expresses many of his suppressed - or repressed - sympathies with the Republican side in that war. In both instances, the attitude is an extension of the guilt motif discussed earlier. (Hugh is also an extension or caricature of some of the young English writers whom Lowry knew, especially the Cambridge underground poet, John Cornford, who was killed in the Spanish Civil War.) Hugh, drunkenly singing revolutionary songs, openly expressing his unsophisticated pro-Spanish Republican attitudes - the Consul calls him an "interior Marxman" - serves to remind the Consul that one can be committed to a cause, - an action impersonal enough even for an inhibited man like Firmin - the second-best thing to loving someone. But Hugh is (like some of the other characters in the novel) another side of himself, the action side, and the Consul is not about to commit himself to any cause, although that would be a moral rather than a physical gesture.

The Spanish Civil War (in particular the crucial Battle of the Ebro) does figure to some extent throughout the novel. Lowry himself had been in Republican Spain in 1933, three years before the outbreak of the Civil War, and had met Jan Gabrial, his first wife, there. The Consul, like Lowry himself, can support the Spanish Republican philosophically, but not politically or ideologically. He, like Lowry, distrusts propaganda of any color or persuasion. He, like Lowry, can also recognize similarities between the Mexican military police and the Guardia Civil, the Spanish fascist police. It is only poetic justice, therefore, that the Consul is inevitably murdered by the secret fascist Mexican police, and the last word that the Consul hears before he dies is companero, comrade, the word used by the Communists in the Spanish Civil War. The Consul, like so many of the other foreign consuls in Latin America, is suspected of being a "spider" or spy by the Mexican police. In any event, Lowry was far from being indifferent to the political and social currents of the 1930s.

Cinema As Technique. The technique of the novel is essentially cinematic. After his stay in Paris and elsewhere, Lowry went to New York for about a year, and then joined his friend John Davenport in Hollywood. He worked on several film scripts (including F. Scott Fitzgerald's *Tender Is the Night*), picked up quite a bit of technical knowledge about film-making, and later applied this knowledge to the writing of *Under the Volcano*. It is therefore no surprise to find Jacques Laruelle, a disillusioned Hollywood film director, serving as one of the key characters in the novel. The book opens with an extended flashback in Laruelle's mind. As he walks along familiar sites, he is reminded of the Consul's death exactly one year ago. He replays, mentally, the sequences which led to the final **catastrophe**. Then there is another flashback, this one to a much earlier time when both he and Firmin were two boys visiting the English poet, Abraham Taskerson.

Still other elements of the cinema come into play. Lowry-Laruelle employs flashbacks within flashbacks, abrupt shifts from sustained scenes to closeups, as though hundreds of exposed feet of movie film had been cut and edited. The film playing at the local movie house is Las Manos de Orlac; just a year ago, it was also playing there. Now the title runs through the novel like a leitmotif. Actually, it wasn't much of a film; it was all about a pianist who imagined that his hands were those of a murderer, and, in the manner of a Lady Macbeth, he kept trying to wash the blood off them (the ever-present guilt motif of the novel). The reader - or viewer - one gathers, is supposed to substitute Firmin for Peter Lorre (the "pianist" in the film) at this point. Firmin feels guilty for the Indian's death because he never tried to help him. He also feels guilty (or might have felt guilty, if he hadn't died first) for Yvonne's death when she was trampled to death by the wild horse (Number 7 on its rump) that he, Firmin, had unwittingly untied. (The guilt motif persists: in October Ferry to Gabriola, Lowry's last novel, Ethan Llewelyn accepts the guilt for the death of a young man whom he had not tried to dissuade from committing suicide.)

In addition to *Las Manos*, other film titles and other phrases recur throughout the novel like subtitles in a foreign-language film - *Cimarron, The Gold Diggers of 1930*, No se puede vivir sin amar, Le Gusta Este Jardin?..., etc.

One therefore expects Laruelle to be preoccupied with cinematic matters (Firmin had suggested to him a possible subject for a film - if Laruelle could ever get himself to work again). But Yvonne also manifests a strong interest in film. She had once been a movie actress. She knows a great deal about the films shown at the local movie house, more than a casual or bored habitual moviegoer would know. Nor is she a mere movie buff; she had been directly involved in the making of many films some time ago.

Lowry himself liked the kinetic quality of films. He himself found it absolutely natural to move or jump from one interest to another - music, golf, jazz, poetry, writing, literature, film-making, etc. - and it was this intellectual restlessness which may have made him appreciate the potentialities of films. A film, Lowry observed, moved in several directions, impervious to time, impervious to the forward (but mechanical) direction taken by the reel of film itself.

One other point: Long before the Japanese film Rashomon, Lowry was aware of the way in which a film could narrate a single event from several points of view. In the novel itself, the reader is given four versions of that one day in November, 1938 - the Consul's Hugh's, Yvonne's and Laruelle's.

Music As Technique. In Chapter VI, Hugh is involved in a long interior monologue in which he reminisces about his earlier career as a song writer. Lowry himself composed some music of consequence too; in any event, he was deeply involved in music, popular and classical, and this side of him is fairly clearly expressed both through Hugh and through the structure of the novel. The four principals in the novel may be said to have been arranged in the form of a string trio (with Laruelle playing a kind of obbligato), with the major motifs or **themes** being played by each of the "instruments" in turn. The arrangement:

Chapter I Laruelle
    II Yvonne
    III Consul
    IV Hugh
    V Consul
    VI Hugh,
    VII Consul
    VIII Hugh
    IX Yvonne
    X Consul
    XI Yvonne
    XII Consul

Such a contrapuntual arrangement serves to show the interplay of thought and action, a natural outcome of shifting character viewpoints. (Lowry himself preferred to describe each of the major motifs sounded through the three main characters as "chords," played, perhaps, on a kind of surrealistic organ.) The Consul is obviously the key player, not exactly the soloist, with Yvonne and

Hugh providing the counterpoint. In essence, what Lowry may have accomplished by this is a musical Rashomon effect.

Lowry once remarked to Conrad Aiken that when he was writing *Under the Volcano*, he felt that the book was writing him. There is no point in trying to challenge that statement.

LITERARY INFLUENCES ON LOWRY

Since he was a prolific reader, it is almost impossible to trace all the literary influences on Lowry. Other non-Mexican writers on Mexico, such as B. Traven or D. H. Lawrence? Practically none at all. Conrad Aiken and James Joyce? Yes. The nineteenth-century Romantics such as Wordsworth, Shelley, and Coleridge? Certainly. The Elizabethan sonneteers and Marlowe? Without a doubt. Sea writers like Melville, Conrad, Dana, and Eugene O'Neill, and to some extent Henry James, Flaubert, Baudelaire, Rimbaud, Dostoevsky, and many others, as is to be expected of a Cambridge University honors graduate. Dante? A seminal influence! As Conrad Aiken put it, somewhat bitterly, "Malc had this way of being admiringly predatory in the using of other men's writing and contrite about it at the same time."

Sea Writers. There are many analogs in *Under the Volcano* (and in the stories "Through the Panama" and "The Bravest Boat") to the beginnings of Lowry's love of the sea - his maternal grandfather (a Norwegian sea captain) and his literary antecedents: Melville, Conrad, and the early Eugene O'Neill. But these three writers (along with Nordahl Grieg, a Norwegian writer of some reputation), although they could provide him with a practicable blueprint of the search for identity through sea voyaging, they could not provide him with a compatible texture, fabric, or frame within which to set the sea voyage as quest. Lowry finally found the blueprint in Aiken's first novel, *Blue Voyage*.

Lowry borrowed from Melville, but only slightly. In *Ultramarine*, the ship is called Oedipus Tyrannus, a self-conscious imitation of the archetypal name of Rights of Man for the ship in Melville's *Billy Budd*. The psychiatrist in Lunar Caustic, Lowry's novella about a drunken derelict in Bellevue Hospital, is named Doctor Claggart, after Melville's villain in *Billy Budd*. But whatever impressive passages there may be in *Ultramarine* are indebted to Joyce (through Aiken), and not to Melville.

In essence, then, Lowry could comprehend the Joyce-Aiken experimentalism, but he couldn't make it work all the way in Ultramarine. There is one exception, however, and that is Dana Hilliot's drunken, disorderly interior monologue in which his drunken fantasy carries him from his mother to a Singapore brothel, then on through a series of Latinate forms of names for God - Zeus, Dis, Dios, Dii, Deorum, Deis, Dais - to his old math teacher, D. S. R. Miles (a closet homosexual), and, finally, to the pseudo-Negro version of a song about the Crucifixion.

The four-page-long passage is probably Lowry's first - and fairly successful - attempt at the use of the stream-of-consciousness device. For a novice writer, it stands up fairly well against Stephen Dedalus' mock sermon at the close of the Oxen of the Sun-Hospital chapter in Ulysses. Lowry, apparently, was an apt pupil - or, Aiken was a very skillful teacher, or both.

Aiken - Preceptor, Mentor, Father-Figure. During his first year at Cambridge University, Lowry read Aiken's *Blue Voyage*. Not only did this book then become for him a literary primer, but Aiken then became in addition a major objective in the life of this twenty-year-old. He wrote to Aiken and pleaded with him to take him on as a literary protege. Aiken consented, and during the first year of their relationship, Lowry completed his first novel, *Ultramarine*.

    As a kind of quid pro quo for the extraordinary tutorial Aiken was affording him, Lowry "posed" for the brilliant dipsomaniac Hambo in Aiken's autobiographic *Ushant*, and in the autobiographical novel, *A Heart for the Gods of Mexico*. Through *Blue Voyage* and subsequent novels in which Aiken exploited the interior monologue and the Joycean stream-of-consciousness device, Lowry became a Joycean once removed. By studying these novels, as well as Aiken's careful analysis of *Ulysses*, Lowry first experienced the Joycean baptism that was eventually to make him a convert (albeit an unwilling - or unconscious - one) to the Joycean process of "evoking consciousness from the flux of life." The chain of influence may be traced from *Ulysses* (published in 1922) to *Blue Voyage* (begun in 1922, published in 1927) to *Ultramarine* (published in 1933) and *Under the Volcano* (begun in 1937 in Cuernavaca in the company of Aiken, himself working on *Ushant*).

    Eventually, and with the help of Aiken, Lowry was able to fashion his own literary technique reminiscent but not imitative of Joyce's. He did this by carefully studying Aiken's experimental application of Joycean devices in *Blue Voyage*. The parallels between Aiken's *Blue Voyage* and Joyce's *Ulysses* are many and easily detected. The Joycean "derivations" in *Under the Volcano* are relatively rare. There is, for example, the tragicomic, grotesque mind trips the Consul takes when his sensibility has been expanded by heroic doses of mescal. Another example is the "garden" scene in Chapter V, comparable in some respects to the Nighttown section in *Ulysses,* mainly because of Lowry's brilliant wordplay.

In the summer of 1929, Lowry left England to visit Conrad Aiken in Cambridge, Massachusetts. Superficially, the purpose was to express in person his admiration for the author of *Blue Voyage*, an admiration expressed earlier and profusely in a letter to Aiken. Lowry spent that whole summer with the Aikens, and entered Cambridge University in the fall of the same year. From 1930 to 1932, the Aikens lived in Rye, Sussex, England, and Lowry was permitted to spend his summer vacations away from the University with them. In 1933, he spent the summer with the Aikens in Spain. During the years 1936–1938, Lowry spent a great deal of time in Mexico with the Aikens.

Much has been written about this beautiful relationship between the brilliant literary novice and the generous, established writer. Lowry sought out Aiken, some critics have said, to escape from his devout Methodist father (Aiken was a bohemian of sorts), to acquire a second, more permissive father, to study at the feet of a literary mentor or guru. In fact, one critic has never tired of describing the Lowry-Aiken relationship as the "Lowry-Aiken Symbiosis." The dictionary defines "symbiosis" as "the intimately living together of two dissimilar organisms especially when mutually beneficial." The evidence hardly makes a case for a genuine quid pro quo that would add up to a symbiotic relationship. True, the two men lived together "intimately" (perhaps "familially" would be a better, less suggestive word); the two men were dissimilar in many respects - age, status, literary development, etc. But it is hard to see how the relationship was "mutually beneficial."

What did Lowry give Aiken in return for the direct - and indirect - instruction he received? Companionship, a drinking partner, a sycophant, an ego support, an overzealous pupil who would flatter any teacher? If all of these were true, would Lowry's "contribution" match what Aiken gave to him (and which we shall detail below)? In view of the unromanticized account of the relationship, parasitism rather than symbiosis may be a more accurate term.

The dictionary defines parasitism as "the intimate association between two or more organisms, especially one in which a parasite obtains benefits from a host which it usually injures." In presenting this unromanticized account below, we intend to make no moral judgments; we offer instead the details of the process whereby Aiken helped Lowry convert the naive, obvious Hambo character of his (Aiken's) two books into the archetypal character of the Consul in *Under the Volcano*.

1. Ushant Oedipally pairs Hambo the son and D., the father seeking to enjoy the wife (Nita) of his son. Compare this relationship with the original Consul-Yvonne-Hugh triangle in the germinal short story *Under the Volcano*, where the Consul is the father, Yvonne, his daughter, and Hugh, Yvonne's lover.

2. In the earlier versions of *Under the Volcano* (short story and first draft of the novel) Yvonne is closely related to the Jan-Nita character whom Lowry-Hambo (in *Ushant*) tries to keep from leaving him by giving her a pair of cheap earrings. In Volcano, Lowry-Hambo becomes Lowry-Hambo-Consul.

3. Nita's "high, spiked, arrogant heels" becomes Yvonne's "high, spiked, arrogant heels" in the earlier version of Volcano. Nita, Hambo's man-teasing wife, becomes Yvonne, ready to sleep with Hugh and Laruelle in Volcano.

4. The intensely violent discussion between the Consul and Hugh in Chapter X of *Under the Volcano* is an accurate

"translation" of the bitter argument between Hambo and D. in *Ushant* over the latter's radically leftist views. In Volcano, the Consul (ne Hambo) takes strong issue with Hugh (ne D.) over Hugh's "indoor Marxmanship," his tepid - and futile - commitment to many of the "people's revolutions" in the 1930s.

5. The acrimonious exchange between the Consul and Hugh toward the end of Chapter VIII in *Under the Volcano* is (according to Aiken himself) a verbal facsimile of a similar argument between Lowry and Aiken in Cuernavaca. Only the positions of the disputants have been reversed, apparently to "protect" the identity of the principal involved.

6. The Consul in the end becomes a symbol of the continuing philosophical and psychological dispute between Lowry and Aiken. The latter, in most of his writings, sought to overcome the "disharmony between man's egotism and unimportance;" to seek, as it were, a viable consciousness in the void. Lowry, for his part, through drink, mysticism, and characters molded in his self-image (especially the Consul), sought salvation and survival in the unconscious. It is only through unconsciousness, however induced, that the Consul finds temporary escape from the "complete baffling sterility of existence as sold to you."

7. At nineteen, Lowry began imagining himself as "half-brother" to Demarest (in Aiken's *Blue Voyage*). He began to see himself as similarly narcissistic, full of self-love and self-pity. The appropriated self-image remained with Lowry for the rest of his life, and pervades almost every piece of writing he did. Take this narcissistic

element out of the Consul's makeup, and what do you have? A severely diminished, albeit more human, more humane individual; and in the end, freed of the Christ or Messiah complex, probably someone who could then make at least one positive gesture toward surviving.

Joyce - Direct Or Indirect Influence? Malcolm Lowry disclaimed any literary derivation from Joyce, and especially from Joyce's *Ulysses*. He first read Ulysses in 1952, five years after the publication of *Under the Volcano*. Lowry did admit, however (in 1951), that he was aware that Joyce considered the name Lowry as something special, that the name occurs in the Hades burial scene in *Ulysses*, and that Joyce had been trying to track down a long poem, *Coming Forth by Day of Osiris Jones*, when he died. All the available published evidence points, nevertheless, to Aiken as the source for Lowry's original knowledge of *Ulysses*.

Nonetheless, The Times Literary Supplement reviewer called *Under the Volcano* "a masterpiece as rich and humorous as *Ulysses* and far more poetic." Another critic saw a complete Homeric parallel in Chapter X of *Under the Volcano*, a parallel more along the lines of Joyce's *Leopold Bloom* than of Homer's *Odysseus/ Ulysses*. Jacques Barzun (in his Harper's magazine review) said that he was unable to digest this "regurgitation" of Ulysses. (In a subsequent letter to Lowry, Barzun admitted that after a second reading, Ulysses was sui generis, and so was *Under the Volcano*.) The New Yorker reviewer needed but one paragraph to label Volcano as "a rather good imitation of an important novel [*Ulysses*]."

But in 1940, Lowry had advised the young Irish writer, James Stern, to avoid in writing a novel not only poems (like Faulkner), conjunctions (like Hemingway), quotations from quotations from other novels, but also inventories (like Joyce). (He might have added: catalogs, like Homer.) And so, most literary scholars and critics have chosen to ignore Lowry's disclaimers and to find *Under the Volcano* "either directly influenced by Ulysses or full of the resonances of that novel"; or to assert that "the writer with whom Lowry has most in common is James Joyce," and that Lowry's stylistic derivations from Joyce are "a critical commonplace." Be that as it may, the "evidence" is at the least coincidental rather than circumstantial, and extrapolated from obvious but unintentional similarities or "resonances."

The "evidence" (better, the direct "testimony" afforded by Aiken) shows that Lowry acquired most of his Joycean influences through Aiken, who was both a contemporary of Joyce's and one of the first of Joyce's "friendly" critics.

The fact remains that Lowry was no youthful Joyce writing *Dubliners* at a correspondingly young age. For one, he lacked Joyce's already mature technique. For another, unlike Joyce, he could not detach himself then (or even afterward) from his characters far enough to provide them with a life apart from his own. Even as early as *Ultramarine*, Lowry was bent on revealing the hero manque, "the man of supreme sensibility who is fallen but does not choose to rise." Joyce, on the other hand, was more interested in the outer rather than the inner world of his main characters. Lowry, with the arrogant ambitiousness of the super-self-confident artist, wanted to make his Consul (and perhaps himself as well) the symbol of a nation invaded and devastated, of man's inhumanity to man, of mankind living without love and unable to accept love. In the end, Lowry's compulsion to justify the ways of man to God was too strong for his extraordinary but still inadequate gifts. Joyce's more modest ambition (to be a writer, not a messiah) never outran his equally extraordinary gifts.

Other Influences. As someone might "read for the law," Lowry "read for the novel." There are traces, resonances, imitations, adaptations in *Under the Volcano* and other books of his of many other writers whom Lowry had read and studied. He knew Hemingway's novels. (By some interesting coincidence, a Malcolm Lowry was host to Ernest Hemingway both in Kansas City and Los Angeles in the early Thirties. This was not the Malcolm Lowry of *Under the Volcano*.) One finds traces of Poe in the very first chapter of Volcano. Lowry must have read both Faulkner and Virginia Woolf in schooling himself in the use of stream-of-consciousness techniques. Kafka's novels must have had much to say to Lowry on modern disoriented man. In fact, considering how much Lowry did read, the relatively slim output of the man seems to lead to but one conclusion: he read much, absorbed much, but assimilated little. And therein, perhaps, lies the explanation for the unfinished, disorganized, but almost totally original nature of his writing.

RELATION OF "UNDER THE VOLCANO" TO LOWRY'S OTHER WORKS

The total body of Lowry's published works is slim. There are, however, thousands of manuscript pages of other works that Lowry had written, or was writing, that have remained unpublished, but, if published, would add considerably to his "credentials" as a modern fiction writer. (Much of this material is in the Lowry collection at the University of British Columbia in Vancouver, Canada.) The fact remains that, on the basis of the published evidence on hand, Lowry must be characterized as a potentially great writer who produced one "accidental" masterpiece, *Under the Volcano*, on which he must be judged.

Ultramarine (1933). This novella is experimental and, as is to be expected of a first book by a young writer, highly derivative (of Aiken, O'Neill, Conrad, and Joyce, by way of Aiken). There is much stream of consciousness (Hilliot's interior monologue in the forecastle, for example), and many examples of contrapuntal rhythms in the manner of O'Neill, particularly in the conversation of the sailors. The conversational counterpoint, similar to a fugue for non-musical voices, reached its peak of expertness later on in *Under the Volcano*.

Dana Hilliot, the hero of the story, is the first of several fictional Lowry characters who will re-enact incidents in the author's own life. Hilliot's trip is a search for manhood, an act of self-recovery. By the end of the trip, Hilliot has still not succeeded in adapting to the universal environment. The sense of isolation - dispossession, eviction, alienation, anomie - eventually becomes the trademark of the other Lowry personae, as of Lowry himself. Kafka (with whose work Lowry was familiar) was probably the first author in modern times to articulate this strange combination of isolation and evil. Still another prototype for Hilliot may be found in Conrad's *The Nigger of the "Narcissus."*

Another datum that was to be developed more extensively in Lowry's later works is to be seen in Hilliot's fear of sex and syphilis, a fear sublimated by the young man in alcohol and masturbation. To protect his virginity from the taunts of his shipmates, he makes much of his promise to Janet (the girl he left behind) to save himself for her, to remain "pure" and faithful.

Hear Us O Lord From Heaven Thy Dwelling Place (1961). This is a posthumously published collection of three short novels and four tales. The three short novels are entitled "Through the Panama," "The Bravest Boat," and "The Forest Path to the Spring." The middle stories are earlier experiments in the novella, imitative of Henry James' handling of complex consciousness, accounts of writers abroad (e.g. Sigbjorn

Wilderness in Rome), other Lowry "doubles," displaced, dispossessed, evicted persons seeking -what? - among the ruins of Pompeii. The other pieces and the long final selection, "The Forest Path to the Spring," are thinly disguised (better, fictionized) accounts of Lowry's honeymoon and life in British Columbia, Canada.

The character Sigbjorn Wilderness, who appears in many of these stories (and 'in *Dark As the Grave Wherein My Friend Is Laid*), was to have been the central figure in *The Voyage That Never Ends*, a sequence of six or seven books planned by Lowry, with *Under the Volcano* the center or keystone. "The Forest Path to the Spring," perhaps Lowry's only completely happy, affirmative work, was actually intended to be the concluding section of the six- or seven-part opus; the final scene of "The Forest Parth" was to be, in fact, the final scene of the whole sequence - Dante's (Lowry's) ascent, as it were, into Paradise.

The seven stories are essentially monologues on travel, memory, art, life, married love, atonement, and mysticism. The monologist is by turns Sigbjorn Wilderness, Kennish Drumgold Cosnahan, or Roger Fairhaven, all Dickensian- named personae of Lowry himself. The woman present in all of these stories is generally Yvonne of Under the Volcano (often Mrs. Margerie Bonner Lowry) made up to resemble somebody else, the name changed "to protect the identity" of the real person.

A discussion of each of the seven stories in the collection follows.

"Through The Panama." The first long story, "Through the Panama," is an account of a sea voyage rich in myths, musical themes, scenery, etc. The story is told in diary form. At the end, the ship is floundering in a violent storm, and the story becomes an almost physically felt account of Everyman's ship on Life's voyage. The entry for December 11, for example, introduced by a quotation from Chaucer, is marginally annotated with excerpts from Coleridge's *The Rime of the Ancient Mariner*. With the safe arrival of the ship at Bishop's Light, England, on December 17, Lowry once again makes use of a quotation from the *Rime*, one of the **didactic**, moralistic quatrains tacked on to the end of that work: "And the Ancient Mariner beholdeth, etc..."

"Through the Panama" is a valuable source of much personal data about Lowry himself. The story is a confessional, true, but the real protagonist is neither Wilderness (a Lowry double) nor Martin Trumbaugh (a Wilderness double); it is man's consciousness, the consciousness of the apprentice-artist of Ultramarine, now grown up to be Sigbjorn Wilderness, or the mature Lowry. Wilderness is Lowry's favorite alter ego, Lowry visualized by Lowry as the deliberately isolated spokesman for mankind. And for this exhortatory effort, Lowry draws upon Coleridge's Ancient Mariner (yet another isolated spokesman for mankind) for marginal commentary, and on a history of the Panama Canal.

Much is made in fact of Coleridge's Ancient Mariner and on his burden of culpability. With a minor borrowing from Conrad's Chance, Lowry equates the effect of the sin of the Mariner with the sense of literary isolation, alienation from his own artistic contemporaries (he is only now first becoming known in Canada, where he spent the ten most productive years of his life); through the involuted Lowry logic, this isolation becomes a Calvinistic conviction of guilt. Lowry now sees himself as one with that famous group of alienated writers - Poe, Kafka, Melville, the early O'Neill - Lowry, the "Ancient Mariner of modern art."

"The Bravest Boat." This is one of three pieces in the collection with a Canadian setting (the other two are "Gin and Goldenrod" and "The Forest Path to the Spring"). The idea for the story came from a Vancouver news item about a bottle set adrift with a note in it. Lowry's version is a lyrical love story about a rootless voyager. A toy boat is set adrift with a note in it written by a boy named Sigurd. Many years later, the boat and the note are found by Astrid, and she marries Sigurd. The story recapitulates all the circumstances which brought the two lovers together.

    First published in France and later in America by Whit Burnett in his magazine Story, "The Bravest Boat" has at least two familiar Lowry benchmarks. First, it draws upon his atavistic affection for his maternal Scandinavian antecedents by using Norse names for his two main characters. Secondly, the sea figures strongly in the location of Enoch was the son of Cain; God made the first garden; Cain Liverpool, England, and never got the salt water out of his blood.) One critic has pointed out that Enochville (possibly a satirical pseudonym for Vancouver) is the city of Enoch; Enoch was the son of Cain; God made the first garden; Cain made the first city. The city then becomes (symbolically and ecologically) God's violated garden (Le Gusta Este Jardin?... Evite Que Sus Hijos Lo Destruyan!) Cain the hijo (son), like the padre (father) Adam, has violated the "garden." But the sea, water, has both a germinative and a purifying effect, and it is Enochville's proximity to the sea that may yet save it from ultimate contamination, corruption, and damnation. At this point, it may be well to compare Lowry's conception of water with T. S. Eliot's in *The Waste Land*. Eliot to be sure was no sea-lover like Lowry. Water, to him, in any form was a signal of God's grace, very closely approximating the holy water of baptism and other rituals. One has no way of knowing, however, how far Lowry wished to proceed on the theological road. We do know how highly he valued water (especially the sea) as a counterbalance to fire (in any shape or form).

The simple charm of "The Bravest Boat," and its freedom from any suggestion of the infernal forces that more commonly beset Lowry and pervade most of his other writing, have justly made it a much-anthologized story. In this respect, it is very untypical Lowry. Lowry, like the two lovers in the story, may have seen, for a very short moment in his own troubled life, that all human destiny is an amalgam of the chaos that can destroy and the faith that can renew. It is almost impossible to conceive that he was not enunciating in much clearer, more human terms, one of the key "mottoes" from *Under the Volcano*; to wit, No se puede vivir sin amar.

"Gin and Goldenrod." Like "The Bravest Boat," this story is a reflection of the rare, happy side of Lowry. It is an anecdotal story built around two of Lowry's favorite personae, Sigbjorn Wilderness and his wife Primrose, as they wander through the narrowing margin between civilization and nature, debris and flowers. Gin in the title represents addiction, a very modern (inside and outside the ghetto) shield against the numbing sterility of urban and suburban dementia. Goldenrod represents a simple, natural antidot to the poison of addiction. (Has there been any pharmacological evidence to this effect? Some species of goldenrod have yielded leaves which have been used for medicinal preparations and teas. The botanical name, solidare, is the Latin for "to make whole." Was Lowry aware of this, or was he merely interested in a neat alliteration?)

The Sigbjorn Wilderness in this story wants to pay off a long-overdue debt to a bootlegger for gin received. Sigbjorn rationalizes that alcoholism is an expected offshoot of the kind of civilization in which we live. Moreover, he further rationalizes (beware of the cockeyed rationalizations of the alcoholic when sober!), if there were no bootleggers available in areas where drinking is prohibited, there would be no reason for drinking prohibited alcohol. (This of course is a transparent variation on the "forbidden fruit tastes sweeter" argument.) In the end, however, even if one were to allow for the relief that "Gin and Goldenrod" affords the reader from Lowry's more persistent gloominess, this story is one to sneeze at.

"Strange Comfort Afforded By The Profession." This is a fairly short short story that is in some respects a prose version or extension of Stephen Spender's poem, "I Think of Those Who Were Truly Great"; (in particular, John Keats) and in more general terms a discussion of the tension between life and art.

Sigbjorn Wilderness (or is it Lowry? But he never actually received any kind of scholarship) is in Rome on a Guggenheim Fellowship. He pauses before the house Keats once occupied in Rome in 1821, just alongside the Spanish Steps. Everything about the house and the adjoining area becomes a fit subject for his voracious notebook. He concludes that an artist must die before he can be appreciated. He identifies himself (and Lowry) with many of other great dead writers. Dying is easy, but what assurance is there that even then a great writer will be appreciated?

The artist's reward, Wilderness eventually confesses, can be found in the precedents of the misery, struggle, and poverty of his predecessors. It is a consolation devoutly to be wished when one is an alienated artist. It may be a fallacious argument in that it suggests that "to suffer is to create"; that the garret is ipso facto more of a guarantee of artistic achievement than the well-appointed townhouse or duplex apartment.

"Elephant and Colosseum." This story is the only example we have of a purely ironic comedy, a sustained joke on Lowry himself. More objective than much of Lowry's other works, it is worth considering as one of the few occasions on which Lowry was able to escape from himself. Kennish Drumgold Cosnahan is a successful writer of a book describing his experiences as a deck hand (or are we after all back to Dana Hilliot in Ultramarine and, inevitably, to the omnipresent Lowry?) on a freighter returning from Singapore. Its main cargo is a collection of animals from Africa and Asia for delivery to European zoos. Outstanding among the many animals is an elephant named Rosemary, whom Kennish had been assigned to watch over. Years later in Rome as a tourist without his wife, and in search of a solution to the "drying up" process which has inhibited his writing, Kennish accidentally wanders from the Colosseum to the zoo where he finds the self-same Rosemary, a survivor of Fascism, war, and defeat. The sight of the elephant ends his artistic block.

"Present Estate Of Pompeii." Roger and Tansy Fairhaven are visiting the ruins of Pompeii. They are neither impressed nor inspired by the scatological graffiti and the brothels. Roger can think only that perhaps a "precious part" of man has disappeared from the earth.

"The Forest Path To The Spring." During June, 1957, Mr. and Mrs. Malcolm Lowry visited Grasmere, Wordsworth's setting for The Prelude. The visit could be construed as an affirmation of Wordsworth's influence (or better, inspiration) on "The Forest Path," a prose poem about man in nature, a "Wordsworthian benediction on nature's benevolent power to transform the heart capable of seeing and receiving." But Lowry could see far beyond the bland pantheism of Wordsworth; a man, who, like Dante, has walked through Hell "does not forget the landscape or the citizenry." And, like Dante, he was able to "establish a symmetrical relationship between the literal and archetypal narrative." In fact, because for once Lowry was able to transcend his self-centeredness, his almost megalomaniacal narcissism, "The Forest Path to the Spring" becomes his most pleasant, satisfying, objectively pure story.

"The Forest Path" was to be the happy, optimistic, soul-elevating ending to the long Dantesque work Lowry had planned to write. If *Under the Volcano* was to be the Inferno, "The Forest Path" was to be the Paradiso. This seventy-page novella was intended to answer the question "Who am I?" first asked by Wilderness-Lowry in "Through the Panama." The "I" is never identified by name in "The Forest Path," merely as "Narrator," merely as a former jazz musician. The narrator had known some jazz greats in his time, but this was to be no memoir recalling the narrator's (or Lowry's) brief sharing of "the aspects of a very real glory" which once belonged to the Louis Armstrongs, the Duke Ellingtons, and the Joe Venutis.

Rather, "The Forest Path" is a Thoreauvian review of the cycle of the seasons. The eight carefully structured sections comprise an objective pastoral, part narrative prose, part poetic prose. Like Thoreau, Lowry was searching for perfection in a life made holy by following the injunction to "Simplify, simplify." The image clusters in "The Forest Path" - animal, floral, water, rain, insect, shelter, time, seasonal rebirth -all suggest that Lowry agreed with Thoreau that "a man is rich in proportion to the number of things he can do without."

If the real antagonist for both Thoreau and Lowry was the world, for Lowry at least the additional antagonist was the overselfed self he had been living with all these years. In "The Forest Path" he was trying to discover (perhaps for the first time in his life) the correspondence between elemental forces and man's "abiding but muted selflessness." (It is very likely that Thoreau, had he lived in Mexico, would have recognized the Mexican natives' discovery and acceptance of this correspondence in terms of living; Lowry, if he was aware of this Mexican form of symbiosis between the elemental forces of nature and man's selflessness, probably saw it in terms of dying.)

Lowry later came to see that, like Thoreau's life before Walden, his life had been a sham, a stage play written, directed, and acted by him, full of empty heroics, mannered gestures, unconvincing apologetics. The **theme** of "The Forest Path" is the narrator's (and Lowry's) attempt at achieving human integration, peace, not a cease-fire, between man's primal urges and fears, and the false buffers that a meretricious civilization throws up against them - "the achievement of oneness with nature against the fatuities of progress."

Had the Consul survived, he might have been recognized in this story as one who was resurrected and reborn through the magic of water as rebirth, purged of all his demons. The narrator's first walk down the path to the spring is a quest for the magical curative powers of water that will quench the fires of hatred that are devouring his life like one great forest fire. The mountain lion he encounters on this first walk is the Dantean symbol of rage, of psychological incontinence that can lead to self-betrayal. The lion turns away, rage disappears, and the narrator (unlike the Consul) finds salvation, a new baptism, from the holy (made holy by Nature, not by theological man) waters of the little spring. With the onset of winter, the path to the spring becomes impassable, but his newly acquired faith can now prod his imagination into taking him to the spring nevertheless. And, like Thoreau, he also knows that "a bucket of water soon becomes putrid, but frozen remains sweet forever." This Keatsian, Platonic truth is most reassuring.

"Our voyaging is only great circle sailing," the narrator's new mentor has told him. (It is interesting to note that Dante's mentor through Inferno and Purgatorio was Virgil, a pagan; that Virgil, a non-Christian, could not serve as his guide through Paradiso. Lowry - or the narrator - for his journey through his Paradiso has finally rejected all his "pagan" mentors and has taken on a Christian guide. But what a Christian! A pantheist, an agnostic, a nonpracticing Christian more closely attuned to the gurus of the East than to the priests of the West!) In "The Forest Path" Lowry has also learned from Thoreau a valuable philosophical - as well as literary - lesson, to wit, every man should try to transcend those human limitations which inevitably mandate that the present should be a mere replay of the past. In other words, if we are to use one of Lowry's favorite motifs, the wheel should turn around and around, but it should also move forward even as it turns cyclically. The world turns full circle on its axis every day; but it also moves in its orbit around the sun. The year is greater - and more important - than the day.

Selected Poems (1962). Almost none of Lowry's poems were published during his lifetime. The **imagery** and subject matter relate to the sea, "nature's storms appealing to the storms of the heart." This is true mainly of the earlier poems. Later, the bars, cantinas, jails, and the general landscape of Mexico become increasingly prominent. There are traces in the poems of the influence of Eliot, Rilke, and Yeats, more so of Hart Crane. Lowry evidently reserved most of his poetic effects for his prose.

Dark As The Grave Wherein My Friend Is Laid (1968). On January 10, 1946, Lowry tried to commit suicide by slashing his wrists. On January 16 of that same year, Lowry and his second wife left for Oaxaca, Mexico, where Lowry hoped to find a Mexican friend of his from his first stay in Cuernavaca with his first wife, Jan, in 1936. The man had been dead for several years. The Lowrys then left for Mexico City via Acapulco the next day. *Dark As the Grave* is the account of this journey, distilled from about 700 pages of notes taken by Lowry on the trip - descriptions, dialogues, copies of signs along the way, random observations, etc. After some seriocomic misunderstandings in

Acapulco and Mexico City, the Lowrys were deported (evicted?) and returned to Canada. (The causes of their deportation were recorded to some extent in an unfinished novel, La Mordida.)

Dark As the Grave was edited as a sort of novel by his widow, Margerie Bonner Lowry, and Douglas Day, his official biographer. It is a symbolic account of the journey, and hardly a literal travelogue. Sigbjorn Wilderness is and is not Malcolm Lowry vacationing in Mexico with his wife. He is at once a modern author and at the same time a Dante or a Virgil on his way down into the Inferno. But Lowry is more than a Dante or a Virgil, because he is going back a second time. He is taken in by Virgil's invitation in *the Aeneid* that facilis descensus Averno (the descent into Hell is easy), and that man cannot resist the temptation to attempt that descent. The hell he descends into is no one else's but his own; nor is he certain that he will be able to get out of hell as easily the second time.

Dark As the Grave professes to be the search for a former Mexican friend, Juan Fernando Martinez (Doctor Vigil in *Under the Volcano*); actually, it is the author's (Wilderness or Lowry - take your choice) search for his self. Wilderness leaves Dollarton with his wife Primrose to visit the locale of *The Valley of the Shadow of Death* (Lowry's first title for *Under the Volcano*) before the book had been accepted for publication. Whether the world (or the publisher) accepts his vision of the world or not, he must at the very least convince his wife of the accuracy - and actuality - of that dark descent into hell.

Wilderness never does find Juan Fernando mainly because all these years he has mistakenly thought of his friend as a symbol of life, of vitality; actually, Juan Fernando was more of a symbol of death. Furthermore, by not too strained an analogy, Juan Fernando, in his role of a messenger for a benevolent credit arm of the Cardenas administration (the Banco de Credito y Ejidal in *Under the Volcano* and in *Dark As the Grave*), he is both the deliverer of payments on horseback into the interior, and also the death-delivering horseman in *Under the Volcano*. In *Under the Volcano*, Hugh's friend, Juan Cerillo, is, like Juan Fernando, first just such a messenger, and then, the murdered Indian. Sigbjorn Wilderness' search for Juan Fernando Marquez is in essence a compulsion to relieve the agonized past, the death of Juan Fernando, for it is in the latter experience that Wilderness will find a kind of absolution.

Dark As the Grave is a near-novel, perhaps better left in its unintegrated shape rather than being patched together into a "novel." It is not a novel - even by today's very loose definition. It is, rather, a gloss, an explication de texte of *Under the Volcano*. It is, moreover, a more extended statement of Lowry's philosophy about the relationship of art to life (adumbrated earlier and more briefly in "Strange Comfort"). Finally, it is a most faithful picture of the mind of a writer while he is in the process of writing. For one critic, *Dark As the Grave* is "a voyage along the knife edge of paranoia."

On the autobiographic - or Lowry - level, we learn in Chapter VII of this near-novel how Wilderness-Lowry tried, unsuccessfully, to get his novel about Mexico published. With this information in our possession, we may safely conclude that *Dark As the Grave*, if nothing else, serves to show us how Lowry succeeded in making art transcend life in order to write a masterpiece (*Under the Volcano*, that is). As indicated earlier, *Dark As the Grave* isn't much more than a rough draft of a novel that its editors should not have decided to publish except as a meticulous gloss on *Under the Volcano*. Students of the novel may appreciate its value as (a) a recording of many of the author's experiences later incorporated (or fictionized) into *Under the Volcano* (and for anyone who hasn't read *Under the Volcano*, the book is almost meaningless), and (b) an expose of Lowry's methods of composition. One other feature of this book may be of special interest to the Lowry fan: Even though the voice is that of Sigbjorn Wilderness, the heart and mind are unmistakably Lowry's. There is little effort made to sustain the persona dodge very long; this is Lowry himself speaking as clearly and as personally as he speaks in his letters. Indeed, it is even more unmistakably autobiographic than *October Ferry to Gabriola*; it is also immensely more satisfying in that for once Lowry's conviction that life is in fact a forest of symbols is finally exposed here without artifice.

Lunar Caustic (1968). Originally called *The Last Address* (1940–41), *Lunar Caustic* was to be part of a trilogy called *The Voyage That Never Ends* (Lowry's magnum opus). *Under the Volcano* was to be the first part (Purgatorio). A third, gargantuan novel called *In Ballast to the White Sea* was to provide the Paradiso. (The incomplete manuscript of Ballast, 1,000 or more pages, was lost when Lowry's house burned down.) The trilogy was to describe the "battering the human spirit takes (doubtless because it is overreaching itself) in its ascent towards its true purpose."

Lunar Caustic was published first in England, in 1968. It is based on Lowry's brief commitment to Bellevue Hospital in New York City in 1934 for alcoholism. The experience first took story form in 1935 under the title *The Last Address*, and was then revised a second time in 1940 under the title *Swinging the Maelstrom*. As was typical of Lowry, this was one of several works "in continual, intermittent progress." The book is important because it exploits the same materials used in *Under the Volcano*: addiction and madness, allegedly in the name of the pursuit of transcendence.

The story is "a kind of median between Heaven and Hell," where "death" (if one survives "it") becomes a "prelude to rebirth." As indicated elsewhere, it is of some importance because it also illustrates (a) how Lowry employed thematic analogs to Melville's Billy Budd, and (b) how drink imbued Lowry with a recharged Messianism. Lowry, when sober, could be as cynical as Laruelle; when drunk, he could be as clairvoyant and Messianic as the Consul.

Bill Plantagenet, the English sailor off the S. S. Lawbill drunkenly wandering through the Lower East Side of New York, is Lowry. The delirium tremens **episode** is vividly recalled in *Under the Volcano*, where Belle Vue becomes the Bella Vista bar. The Doctor Claggert in the hospital, along with much of the marine **imagery**, suggests that Melville was the controlling influence in this book (as Richard Henry Dana - cf. Dana Hilliot - may have been in *Ultramarine*).

October Ferry To Gabriola (1970). This book continues - and concludes, since it was Lowry's last piece of writing - the account of the struggle between the transcendent spirit and the threat of eviction first enunciated so beautifully in "The Forest Path to the Spring." But, unlike that book, it contains too many of the Inferno elements (the ever-recurring fires, for example) to serve as yet another element in the Paradiso counterbalance to *Under the Volcano*. In Ethan Llewelyn, the chief character and easily identifiable Lowry persona (although for once the persona is not a writer writing a book), we are introduced to a guilt-ridden individual almost as perplexed as the Consul. In a series of flashbacks covering a one-day bus ride, we learn that he feels guilty for (a) having possibly caused one person to commit suicide by not taking steps to dissuade him, and (b) having as a lawyer in all good conscience secured the acquittal of a client who later proved to be guilty of committing the murder for which he had been exonerated.

The novel, although based on an actual trip taken by the Lowrys in 1946, is set in 1949. The advantage of a postwar perspective gained thereby is obvious, although it is not fully exploited. It does, however, vividly depict the fires raging within and around Ethan Llewelyn. Ethan, like Lowry, is a bit of a shlemazl too, and "The element [fire] follows you around, sir" is applicable to him as readily as it is to Lowry. The inexplicable fires that plague Ethan must be his punishment for the two errors of omission as a lawyer, he finally concludes. And for him, as for the Consul (and for Lowry himself), redemption is nowhere in sight. There is no possible escape from the fires, be they caused by man's carelessness or by some dark retributive force. The fiery parallels between *October Ferry* and *Under the Volcano* are all-too-consciously contrived. As the Llewelyns run away from the fires to Vancouver on the other side of the continent, they see a fisherman's shack burning. As Yvonne lies dying under the horse's hoofs, she thinks of how she and Geoffrey might escape to their other home in that Northern Paradise; but the house, and everything else in their lives, was on fire. And the Consul's last vision is of the world itself on fire, "villages catapulted into space," the pandemonium of a million tanks, and himself falling "through the blazing of the million bodies, falling into a forest..." The Consul's world is coming to an end, not with a bang, not with a whimper, but with the darnedest fire you'd ever want to see. The universal volcano is erupting. The Gotterdammerung is here and now, more spectacular than Wagner could ever have conceived it in his most extravagant dreams.

Ethan is sure that the fires are the pyromaniac Devil's way of punishing him for causing the suicide of young Peter Cordwainer twenty years ago to the day (this day, October 7 - Ethan is also a bit of a Cabbalist - on which they are traveling to Gabriola), and for the greater sin of having failed both God and man, as well as one individual named Peter Cordwainer. Ethan, like the Consul, conceives of his own specific guilt as synonymous with man's universal guilt.

As has already been illustrated, *October Ferry to Gabriola* shares many artistic and textual elements with *Under the Volcano*: all the action takes place within one day; the fire motif; the flashbacks and other cinematic devices; the main character's assumption of man's universal guilt for man's inhumanity to man; the pivotal bus ride; the sense of being dispossessed; Cabbalism and other forms of black - and white - magic; excessive drinking, etc. It lacks, however, what one critic has called "the final expurgatory look," the innate force that *Under the Volcano* possessed in order to achieve the final magnificent "epiphany." But then, Ethan is no Geoffrey Firmin, Canada is not Mexico, and gin (or any other Anglo drink) is not mescal. And Lowry, ten years older and somewhat chastened after his extraordinary "Season in Hell" (like Dante, who, people said, had the look of one who had been in Hell) "could galvanize his vision but once."

Eridanus, the Canadian "paradise," is in some sense (topographically, geographically, geologically) merely a mountainous northern extension of the Mexican volcanic "hell." Gabriola is an island in the Gulf of Georgia between Nanaimo and Vancouver. We can guess that Lowry must have immediately reacted first of all to the word "gulf" through the process of word association which is more highly developed in writers than in laymen (cf. Joyce's word play in Ulysses, and the Consul's extraordinary plays on the word "cat" in Chapter V). "Gulf" is the barraca, "gulf" becomes "golf" in the golf-course images ("Hell Bunker" for example), "Gulf" then suggests the image of a floating island within it. Ethan (or Lowry) is now an Odysseus figure exiled from Paradise looking upon the floating island as a potential haven. At this point Neoplatonism takes over from geography to suggest that the north is the region of the intellect, the south is the region of the senses (Mexico?), the west is the region of the demons, and the east is the region of the gods. Ethan's triangular trip is essentially the course or thrust of the novel. The trip southwest to Victoria represents the alienating mental exile that is Ethan. The bus ride north to Nanaimo signals his return to intellectual awareness; the ferry trip east from Nanaimo to Gabriola gives promise of the peace of mind that only the gods can provide.

Geography, however, is not enough, either for Ethan, the Consul, or Lowry. All three mistakenly seek paradise in a physical climate, when it is the mental climate they need. "Which way I fly is Hell; myself am Hell" said Milton. "And in the lowest depth a lower deep/Still threat'ning to devour me opens wide,/To which the Hell I suffer seems a Heav'n" (*Paradise Lost, IV*).

Next to *Under the Volcano*, *October Ferry* to Gabriola is Lowry's most intellectualized book. "Gabriola may not be the artistic triumph I sometimes think it is," Lowry wrote in 1953, "but if I have any knowledge of the human psyche at all it is...a psychological triumph of the first order..." Lowry drew more extensively than ever on the techniques of film and on images associated with film. "...the eerie significance of cinemas in our life..." "Ethan exclaims. There are constant flashbacks, reruns, in the form of recurrent flower names, references to lighthouses, farolitos, Archangel, abysses, volcanoes, all sorts of residences, signs and portents, magazine articles, etc. "Symbols are pointed out blatantly instead of being concealed or subsumed in the material," Lowry admitted, "or better still simply not there at all..."

The Llewelyns' predicament becomes society's. The whole world is beginning to fear eviction, and October Ferry, like *Under the Volcano*, becomes at one level a social commentary. "Much more profoundly it is a study of Everyman's soul," a Canadian critic wrote. "Outward bound for Gabriola, man is also bound to it; it is his cross and salvation together."

UNDER THE VOLCANO

INTRODUCTION

No technical or critical analysis of *Under the Volcano* can be made without acknowledging the enormous amount of assistance Malcolm Lowry himself provided in the letter to his British publisher, Jonathan Cape, from Cuernavaca, Mexico, on January 2, 1946. The letter is in essence a "brief" submitted in defense of having the novel published much as the author had written it.

GENERAL CONSIDERATIONS

The novel can be read as a story, or "listened to" as a kind of symphony (see below Lowry's explication of themes, chords, variations, etc., all in the language of musical composition), or even as an opera (Lowry jokingly conceded that some readers might even call it a "horse opera"). It is a tragedy and a comedy. It is a song and also a poem. (Lowry was both a poet and a songwriter.) It is "hot" music. (Lowry was a jazz aficionado.) It is a cryptogram. (Cf. Lowry's use of the Cabbala and other esoteric sources.) It is a prophecy and a political warning. (The Spanish Civil War is a conspicuous part of the backdrop against which the tragicomedy is played out.) It is a "preposterous movie" (more later on Lowry's use of cinematic techniques in the novel itself). According to one's taste, the novel can be any one of these; according to Lowry's taste and intention, the novel is all of these.

Garden Of Eden **Theme**. The basic theme of the novel is the Garden of Eden myth. In this allegory, the Garden represents the world from which we are all in more or less danger of being evicted. (One of the universal **themes** that run through almost all of Lowry's works is that of the evicted, the dispossessed, the alienated, the exiled, the expatriated.)

In Lowry's use of the Garden of Eden **theme** or motif, most of the possible implications are exploited - the mythical, the biblical, the religious, the moral, the psychological, etc. Without acknowledging the fact, it is very likely that Lowry used, for one of his many "texts," Iago's speech in Othello (I, iii, 322–337) on gardens:

> **Virtue! a fig! 'tis in ourselves that we are thus or thus. Our bodies are our gardens, to the which our wills are gardeners; so that if we will plant nettles, or sow lettuce, set hyssop and weed up thyme, supply it with one gender of herbs, or distract it with many, either to have it sterile with idleness, or manured with industry, why, the power and corrigible, authority of this lies in our wills. If the balance of our lives had not one scale of reason to poise another of sensuality, the blood and baseness of our natures would conduct us to most preposterous conclusions: but we have reason to cool our raging motions, our carnal stings, our unbitted lusts, whereof I take this that you call love to be a sect or scion.**

Why Mexico? The symbol that Lowry chose for the Garden of Eden is Mexico. Why Mexico? Because it is the eternal battleground of every sort of racial and political conflict. Because its natives observe a religion that is unmistakably death-oriented (all of the action of the novel occurs between the hours of 7 a.m. and 7 p.m. on the Day of the Dead, a religious holiday falling out on November 2). Mexican folklore is extraordinarily preoccupied with death. Some Mexican Indian tribes still believe that the souls of the newly dead take an elaborate seven-day journey involving a trial descent into the darkness of the abyss (hell?). In Chapter I, Laruelle, overlooking the barranca (ravine, abyss), reflects on the Consul's downward journey from 7 a.m. to 7 p.m., all the way through to his downward plunge into the abyss in Chapter XII. Geoffrey's route follows the one outlined by Dante: hell is at the narrow end of a conical pit at the center of the cosmos (cf. also Homer's Hades and Virgil's Avernus). Here one can find Satan, but only after one has discovered the secret path where heaven and hell meet, where God and Satan are one. To understand this is to understand why Geoffrey joyfully exclaims on the way to Parian: "I like hell." Mexico, therefore, becomes a logical place in which to set the drama of a man's struggle between the powers of light and darkness.

Mexico can also be seen as the world itself, or the Garden of Eden, or the world and the Garden as one. Mexico is (or was) geographically remote from us, that is, from the Northern or Western or Anglo world, Mexico is the underside of our world, our "underworld," as it were. Consequently, Mexico may also be construed as a kind of timeless, neutral, ahistorical image of the world. In Mexico, therefore, we can locate the Garden of Eden, or any other mythic place we wish. Mexico is "paradisal: it is unquestionably infernal," Lowry said. The first chapter in particular serves to establish the mood and tone of the novel, as well as the "slow melancholy tragic rhythm of Mexico itself - its sadness - and above all establishes the terrain..."

Le Gusta Este Jardin? *Under the Volcano* is an allegorical enactment of one of the two primal myths of Western civilization, the Fall and Eviction of Adam from the Garden of Eden (Faust is the other myth.) As the novel proper opens in Chapter II (Chapter I is a Prologue in the form of an Epilogue), Geoffrey's garden, deprived of the tender care of the divorced and departed Yvonne, is now a veritable jungle. Yvonne returns, tries to restore the garden (and herself, by the way) to its former purity and innocence, is distracted by Hugh, and finally gives up trying to effect a reconciliation with Geoffrey in the now-hopeless garden. The situation, as the Consul reviews it with Mr. Quincey, his disapproving surrogate God next door, represents both mythic structure and sexual conflict. Is it possible, the Consul asks his neighbor, that Adam was left sole, impotent tenant "presiding over the primal wasteland"? Is it also possible, he adds, that man's original sin was to become a property owner?

Lowry expands and embellishes the basic allegory by introducing two literary explorers of hell as guides for his expelled Adam: Dante, in the dark wood (Casino de la Selva, El Bosque) preparing to descend into the Inferno (barranca); Dr. Faustus, having bartered his soul away for a new and more powerful magic (cf. the Consul's dabbling in Cabbalism), preparing to enter hell in payment for his part of the bargain with the devil. Like the exuberant Faustus, the Consul also loves hell. "I can't wait to get back there," he calls out to Yvonne and Hugh, as he hastens toward the final circle of his descent.

The "Le Gusta Este Jardin?" sign (in line with the Garden allegory, thus becomes the motto of the novel) is mistranslated by the Consul, although it can be translated more accurately by anyone with a fair knowledge of Spanish. The most compelling (because closer to the controlling allegory or **metaphor** of the novel) translation is that provided by Sigbjorn Wilderness (Lowry) in

Dark As the Grave: Does this garden which is His please you? Prevent His sons from destroying it!" This fits in so well with the Consul's allegorical or mythic role of Man, having betrayed the Mysteries entrusted (but unrevealed) to him and having rejected salvation, being expelled from the garden to wander eternally without hope of atonement or redemption (although the Consul does suggest that he, in his post-hell, Popocatepetl-achieved state, will be Man's atoner and redeemer). And, of course, by coincidence or literary intention, it is actually the Chief of Gardens, who officiates at the Consul's execution (or assassination).

The "Real" Garden. Since the actual locale of *Under the Volcano* is the city of Cuernavaca (Quauhnauhuac), Lowry evidently made use of some of the conspicuous features of that place. For example, there is an actual Casino de la Selva there, as well as a barranca, and, particularly, the Borda Gardens, on the Avenidas Morelos e Hidalgo. A recent travel book tells us that it was once occupied by the Emperor Maximilian and Carlotta; that it is now (and was, even as recently as 1968, when we saw it) rundown, virtually untended for a century or so; that it still retains its indolent charm...acres of decaying splendor - "abandoned flower beds, crumbling steps, roofless rooms, esplanades leading nowhere, empty pools and fountains, replete with birds, foliage, flowers, and sleeping peacefully in the somnolent sun, like a forgotten Southern plantation." Except for the unfortunate analogy with a Southern plantation at the end, the description may well be applied to the Consul's garden (with him and Yvonne re-enacting the roles of Maximilian and Carlotta; Lowry does make the comparison himself several times throughout the novel), or to the Garden of Eden - or Mexico - with Maximilian - and Carlotta re-enacting the roles of the dispossessed Adam and Eve.

Drunken Bliss. Although the main character in the novel is unquestionably an alcoholic, a dipsomaniac, a souse, a compulsive drinker, Lowry insisted that the novel (unlike Charles Jackson's The Lost Weekend, for example) was not about drunkenness - at least in the very narrow sense of that word. The chronic drunkenness of the Consul symbolizes the "universal drunkenness of mankind" before or during World War II, a drunkenness or unawareness or unconcern first manifested in the Western world's hands-off policy in the Spanish Civil War. Mankind is afraid of itself; mankind is overwhelmed by the weight of its guilt; mankind is involved in a ceaseless struggle to reach the light "under the weight of the past." Through drunkenness, mankind (and the Consul) becomes narcotized, for a time at least.

The external world of nature represents the inner states of consciousness; the Consul's drunken bliss is reflected in his idyllic, almost reverential, descriptions of the several cantinas. Most of the supernatural (astrological, magical, spiritual) components are held together by the central image of ritualistic or initiatory wine, especially mescal, which possesses the property of divine and demonic communication - or the capacity for effecting hallucinogenic, mind-expanding experiences. In contradistinction to the Consul's drunken bliss, there is his anguish, symbolized by the dogs, vultures, and weed-ridden gardens.

Don't Drink The Water. Many literary critics are essentially literary imperialists in that they tend to examine every other culture almost exclusively in terms of their own culture. The culture of Mexico is an integral part of the total literary and psychological construct of *Under the Volcano*. It brings out all the hidden faults and weaknesses of the Consul. True, he was a heavy drinker even before he came to Mexico, but that "addiction" was to beer, wine, "European" whisky. Note what happens to Firmin when he begins to drink tequila and mescal. He suddenly acquires a "translucent clairvoyance, perfected expression."

"It's the tourist, the outsider, the invader who can't drink the Mexican water without becoming sick; the natives on the other hand experience no ill effects from drinking the water. It is also of considerable importance that the "discomfort" experienced by the foreigner in Mexico is popularly called "Montezuma's (Moctezuma's) Revenge." The Spaniards came to Mexico as "tourists" too. History shows that even after almost 400 years, the Spanish culture hasn't succeeded in overpowering the native Mexican culture. If Cortez - and Maximilian - couldn't find peace in Mexico, why should the Consul have been able to do so? In short, the Consul should not have drunk the "water" - "honey water," the Aztecs called mescal.

Numerology. The book is divided into 12 chapters because the very form and structure of the novel must be visualized as a wheel with twelve spokes. The motion of this wheel (or other wheels mentioned in the novel) is to be conceived as something like time itself. The number twelve to Lowry signified many things: a universal unit; twelve hours in a day (or twelve hours in a night, if we can conceive of a perpetual equinox); twelve months in a year (but not twelve lunar months); the novel is enclosed by a year (November 2, 1939 back to November 2, 1938.) But, most significantly, the number twelve is of the highest symbolic importance in the Cabbala (the twelve signs of the zodiac, the twelve months of the year, and the twelve human activities of seeing, hearing, smelling, tasting, touching, copulating, dealing, walking, thinking, becoming angry, laughing, and sleeping), and Lowry employs the Cabbala for poetical reasons as well (and as his cryptogram?) because it represents man's spiritual aspiration. (Actually, Cabbalistic cosmology includes 3 and 7 as well as 12 among its significant numbers. Lowry makes extensive use of the number 7.)

Each of the twelve chapters (according to Lowry) is also intended to represent a degree in the twelve stages of initiation. Added to this is the symbolic value of each tarot card suit (cf. T. S. Eliot's use of tarot cards in The Waste Land) expressed through (1) wands - Geoffrey's ever-present walking stick; (2) cups - the drinking **theme**; (3) swords - the razor, especially in the scene where Hugh shaves Geoffrey, and the machete: (4) pentacles - the zodiac.

Wood(s). Wood or woods is a thematic symbol in the novel. The book opens in the Casino de la Selva in Quauhnauhuac. (There is an actual Casino de la Selva in Cuernavaca, the "modern" name for Quauhnauhuac. The tourist guidebooks locate it at Leandro Valle 26. "A trip to the Casino de la Selva is worthwhile," we are told, "if only to inspect the grounds, the buildings... With its random selection of plants, trees, pools and stairways [all indoors]... Also offers good jazz..." Lowry, about ten years earlier: "No one ever seems to swim in the magnificent Olympic pool. The springboards stand empty and mournful...") Selva is a Spanish word for wood(s). In Chapter VI, the wood is again referred to in the quotation of the opening lines from Dante's Inferno: "Midway in this our mortal life, I found myself lost in a gloomy wood,/Far off from the direct path..." Wood is mentioned again in Chapter VII, where Firmin enters the cantina El Bosque, a Spanish word for wood or woods (cf. "bosky dell" in English). Finally, in Chapter XI we read about Yvonne's death in the woods, this time real, dark woods.

Under the Volcano draws extensively on Dante. The book is intended to be a kind of Inferno, one of a trilogy, with the other two "books" to come to provide the Purgatorio (Lunar Caustic) or "Through the Panama" and the Paradiso ("The Forest Path to the Spring"). In Chapter VI, the middle or "heart" of the novel, we find Hugh in the middle of his life. He recalls the very first lines from Inferno (see above) as the chapter opens. Dante (or Hugh, or Everyman) finds himself midway in his life in a dark wood. Other Dantesque passages are interspersed throughout the rest of the novel.

Music. Lowry's musical aspirations - and modest accomplishments - can be traced throughout the structure of the novel. He thought of *Under the Volcano* as a symphony - Tragique? Pathetique? Fantastique? - and frequently used the jargon of musical composition in describing the development of (and variations on) the several **themes** first stated in the opening chapter. Mention of the Casino de la Selva in Chapter I "strikes the opening chord of the Inferno," he said. "...this chord being struck again in VI...the chord is struck again...in VII...the chord is resolved in XI..."

Barranca. The barranca is at the base of the volcano (the volcanic peak usually represents the home of the gods). It is the cavernous abyss that represents hell. (The tourist guidebook locates the barranca on the east side of Cuernavaca. It was at one time "a bustling hive of cantinas, rusty motor car parts, corrugated iron huts housing dozens of people, and piles of garbage." The reader should keep his eye on that wrecked blue Ford mentioned in Chapter I.) According to ancient Indian myth, the barranca split open on the day of Christ's crucifixion. (Did it split open again on November 2, 1938, to receive another "crucified Christ" - the Consul? A consul in political or administrative terms is a surrogate for a higher, more powerful ruler. Christ, then, may be construed as God's "consul" or surrogate on earth. Another interesting sidelight to keep in mind: In referring to his imminent, inevitable death, the Consul says, "Es inevitable la muerte del Papa," "The Pope must die." The Pope is Christ's vicar, Christ's consul on earth. So Firmin-Pope becomes, as it were, another consul or vicar of Christ on this earth.)

The barranca is also analogous to the "Hell Bunker" of Geoffrey's first approach to sexual experience. It is the hell (the barranca and the "Hell Bunker") which both attracts and repels him. The barraca is, finally, his grave; it is also symbolic of his separation from Yvonne.

Characters As Symbols. Geoffrey's destruction may represent the coming war (World War II) and the destruction of nations in that war. Hugh's long-overdue commitment to the fight against fascism forecasts America's entry into the anti-fascist war, after her deplorable non-intervention policy in the Spanish Civil War. Yvonne's barrenness (one baby lost, her inability to conceive again, with Geoffrey), her denial of femininity (Lowry the premature male chauvinist!), symbolizes the destructive nature of modern, liberated woman.

The name Geoffrey (Teutonic) means "God's peace" or "peace of the land," and he ironically dies for just that. Firmin (Anglo-Saxon) means "a traveler to distant lands." Hugh (Teutonic) means "mind" or "intelligence." Yvonne (French) is an "archer," or, in Lowry's words, "the eternal woman - angel and destroyer both." Laruelle (French) translates as narrow passage, alley, or small gap between a bed and a wall; he is the archetypal seducer (he is later symbolized by a serpent). Doctor Vigil (a cognate of Virgil, Dante's guide through hell and purgatory) symbolizes a "guardian"; also, as a doctor, his sign, the caduceus (also carried by Mercury, the messenger of the gods) illustrates his other functions, that of guide and master of initiation (after Chapter VII, when the Consul is no longer an "initiate," Doctor Vigil disappears from the novel).

UNDER THE VOLCANO

STYLE AND METHOD

Other works by Lowry show his method of composition in additional detail: five, ten, or even twenty versions of a sentence, paragraph, or chapter would be worked on simultaneously; some of these were completed, others were left to be "completed" or collated by his widow and editors. In his letter to Jonathan Cape (January 2, 1946) Lowry himself provided the key to the careful working of his imagination in the composition of *Under the Volcano*.

There were five separate drafts of the manuscript: (1) the typescript of the germinal short-story version; (2) 364 pages of typescript, already divided into the significant number of chapters, twelve; (3) a clearer, slightly larger (404 pages) version in which the key change in the interrelationships of the Consul, Yvonne, and Hugh have not been made: Hugh, from Yvonne's suitor to the Consul's half-brother; Yvonne, from the Consul's daughter to the Consul's wife. This version is commonly referred to as the first completed, or Mexican, version, and the one offered to publishers (and rejected) in 1940–41; (4) interlinear changes (of new interrelationships of main characters) now penciled in; (5) the "public" or published version, issued in 1947.

Lowry has been compared with other myth-makers, in particular Joyce and Faulkner. Like Faulkner especially, the would-be poet as novelist, he obviously found it difficult to resist writing a prose heavily allusive in texture, and full of "resonances" of the great poets.

A Lowry novel, said Conrad Aiken, was very much like a patchwork quilt put together from random pieces of esoterica that he had found in his vast reading. From Aiken himself, Lowry picked up many Joycean devices such as word-spinning (but not Joyce's kind of glossolalia), inspired punning (also some of T. S. Eliot's extraordinary ironic punning - paradox, irony, ambiguity); and "the controlling device of great circling."

Lowry's genuine familiarity with music must have led him to transmute Richard Wagner's use of musical leitmotifs into the elaborate weaving of literary leitmotifs in *Under the Volcano*. Other aspects of musical composition are clearly evident in the novel. It is these musical devices, as well as some of the cinematic ones, that helped produce in *Under the Volcano* "the tightly bound allegory...a system of abstract equivalents for all the concrete materials of the story."

ORIGINS OF THE NOVEL

Lowry wrote a short story called "Under the Volcano" in 1936. The story is about a visit to the Fiesta at Chapultepec by a Consul, his daughter Yvonne, and her fiance Hugh. While the three are riding on the bus, the bus is suddenly stopped. The passengers get out to see the body of an Indian on the roadside, slowly dying from a wound in his head. Nobody makes a move to help the Indian because, under Mexican law, whoever touches a victim immediately becomes an accessory after the fact.

Earlier in the trip, the Consul, drunk as usual, had noticed with suspicion a fellow passenger, an Indian, also drunk. Was the Consul merely manifesting the traditional fear of the exotic, the latent racism of the Anglo or white for the dark-skinned peoples of his earth? Actually, after the encounter with the dead Indian, the Consul notices that this same fellow passenger, a pelado (that is, one who has been "peeled" of all honor and scruples) has stolen the dying man's few pesos. In effect, a pelado is someone so poor that he will not hesitate to rob his fellow poor. The pelado pays his bus fare with the stolen money. Later, at the Fiesta, the pelado saunters into a pulqueria, ready to spend the rest of the stolen money on more drink.

In the novel, published roughly ten years later (but begun about 1937 in Mexico), these two important changes were made: Yvonne is now the Consul's wife, and Hugh is the Consul's half-brother, but still the Consul's rival of sorts for Yvonne. The father-daughter relationship is significant in light of the Consul's reluctance or inability to come to intimate terms with his wife. The reasons why Hugh must now be a half-brother of the Consul (why not a full brother?) rather than a non-familial total stranger in order to qualify as a rival for his wife's affections, suggest still another ambivalent aspect of Geoffrey's personality. His personality, as filtered through his "other selves" - Laruelle, the murdered Indian, the pelado - is at the least schizophrenic, and it is this fragmented personality that provides the cornerstone of the novel. The Consul brought his fragile personality with him to Mexico; it was Mexico itself, however, that completed the actual fragmentation.

LANGUAGE

Aside from the metaphorical language in which the novel is unquestionably rich, Lowry has a tendency to throw his erudition and extensive reading around with relative abandon. First, there are the more familiar words that he uses excessively: Cabbala, demon, diabolic, spell, infernal, mystery, esoteric, talisman, luck, chance, coincidence. Then there are the perfectly good but extremely uncommon English words that are all-too-redolent of the unabridged Oxford English Dictionary. For example: arcature, tabid, winze, coquelicot, imbricated, cohabation, alkahest, prescinded, horripilating, eclampsia, bartizan, machicolation, merlon, and cucumiform.

There are also the long, non-stop sentences that Lowry is fond of; not the Faulknerian type with little or no punctuation, but the Henry Jamesian kind, extensively and carefully punctuated. A few of the choicer exhibits may be found on pp. 22–23 ("The car halted...was the Con-Sul..."); p. 37 ("It is a light blue moonless summer evening...in the blue evening, unearthly..."); pp. 68–69 ("She might have said yes for once,"..."she does not and cannot appreciate."); pp. 154–55 ("He had not played... and accusing."); pp. 292–93 ("How many bottles...of beautiful mescal"); pp. 349–51 ("Her body was Yvonne's too...what have I done?" 2 1/2 pages long!).

In addition, there are incomparable passages of sustained, inspired prose, among these the long section from Yvonne's interior dialogue on pp. 261–64; the Consul's running commentary on the action in the bullring, pp. 273–274; the description of the interaction between mescal and rainbows, p. 286; the Consul's catalogue of the chemical elements that are against him, p. 304; the Consul's "original" **sonnet**, his Last Will and Testament, p. 330; Yvonne's dying vision and the attack by the horse, pp. 334–45; the Consul's catalogue of the bottles, pp. 292–93.

One may also admire the several examples of beautiful **imagery** Lowry is often capable of producing. For example, this is England, impotent Albion: "the muted voice of England long asleep" (p. 90); "If the paths of glory lead but to the grave - I once made such an excursion into poetry - then Spain's the grave where England's glory led" (p. 104); "But to an Englishman it's such terribly bad form to be a bona fide martyr" (p. 328). Other interesting images: "Hugh put one foot up on the parapet and regarded his cigarette that seemed bent, like humanity, on consuming itself as quickly as possible" (p. 101); "...a crimson and white turkey, a pirate attempting to escape under full sail" (p. 98); "...the little plane of the Compania Mexicana de Aviacion had ascended, like a minute red demon, winged emissary of Lucifer" (p. 44); tourists - "vandals in sandals looking at the murals" (p. 211); impotence of the Consul - "...or falling in a single golden line as if in the act of conceiving a God, falling like a lance straight into a block of ice - (p. 90).

Because *Under the Volcano* may be construed as one great "hallucination," its style is heavily impregnated with the language of hallucinatory experiences - symbolism, condensation, distortion, displacement - all familiar to the characteristics of dreams as categorized by the psychoanalysts. In the interior dialogues especially, the reader may find that "alcoholic hallucinations, trance states, bits of external reality are superimposed onto travel brochures, cinema posters, billboard announcements - all of these somehow merging into a complex symbolic substructure." (Perle Epstein)

STRUCTURE

Reference has already been made to Lowry's fondness for numerology, with especial consideration for the numbers 7 and 12. The novel itself is organized into twelve chapters. Several explanations have been offered by critics and Lowry himself for favoring twelve chapters. A still further explanation may be found in the Aztec Calendar Stone, with which Lowry was known to be familiar. In the center of this stone is the solar face of the Aztecs' principal deity, the sun-god Tonatiuh. His tongue is seen protruding in the form of an obsidian knife, symbolizing his hunger for human sacrifice. The image is surrounded by four squares, symbolizing the four seasons, the four elements (air, earth, fire, water), and the four cosmic ages, or "Suns," through which, according to Aztec belief, the world had passed at the time (1427–79 A.D.). Four (squares) X three (seasons, elements, "suns") gives us the magic number 12.

So much for the twelve-chapter organization of the novel. Exception, however, has been taken by some critics to the unconventional manner in which Lowry has used the first chapter as an epilogue, instead of a prologue, to the action that follows in the succeeding eleven chapters. From the very first pages, for example, we learn that the two main characters, the Consul and Yvonne, are dead. The critical objections to such an opening may be answered as follows: First, the past is prologue, and in that sense, we have an epilogue that is operatively a prologue. Secondly, since this is not a mystery novel, why hide the fact that the two main characters are already dead, and have been dead for exactly one year?

Another objection raised is that the opening chapter comprises a series of flashbacks, albeit ingenious ones. Here again, one can cite other novels which have made extensive use of flashbacks - Proust's *Rememberance of Things Past*, Evelyn Waugh's *Brideshead Revisited*, and others. But the main answer to this criticism is that Lowry, a film writer and film aficionado, chose to use the cinematic technique, and since Laruelle was himself a former film-maker, why not let him logically "stage" these flashbacks? Anyone at all familiar with modern film techniques knows how common - and popular - the flashback is in film today. Then again, one can draw a fairly convincing analogy between the flashback and the psychoanalytic method. In the final analysis, however, Laruelle is merely playing the film reel backward; hence the flashbacks in the form of "film clips."

Lowry himself explained this not-so-radical departure from conventional fiction by emphasizing "the weight of the past," under which terrified, guilt-ridden modern man must struggle to live. In Chapter I, we are introduced to people obviously possessed - and obsessed - by the past: Geoffrey Firmin, ex-consul; Hugh Firmin, ex-newspaperman and ex-Republican partisan in the Spanish Civil War; Yvonne, ex-child film star and Geoffrey's ex-wife; Laruelle, ex-film director, ex-friend of the Consul, and ex-lover of Yvonne. With the end of Chapter I, the time-machine device - "backward revolved the luminous wheel" - which Lowry uses, easily carries us backward in time to a year ago, and from Chapter II on, we are now able to follow the characters within a different time frame. In short, the whole "strategy" of the book is circular - the wheel motif, the twin church towers, etc.

INDEX OF IMPORTANT SYMBOLS

Lowry once remarked that "Life is a forest of symbols, as Baudelaire said, but I won't be told you can't see the word for the trees here." Symbols and myths may be used to create an objective, impersonal world conveniently removed at a decent distance from the writer. So, Yeats created and wore an impersonal ironic mask. So did Eliot and Pound. Joyce joined them in inventing a modern "objective" literature; that is, writing which is "an escape from," not "an expression of," personality. This kind of writing has to be completely free (if at all possible) of any autobiographic, subjective elements. Eliot called this approach the "Objective Correlative."

Lowry uses symbols and myths in a manner totally different from Joyce's or Eliot's or Pound's. He uses them to create the interior world of the Consul. In effect, it can be said of the Consul that "his cosmos was all ego." In *Under the Volcano*, the myth and symbol are used, not as mysterious or metaphoric centers of a time past, but as signposts and representations of the times in which he, Lowry -and the Consul - are living. What the Consul sees is what he is, and everything he sees - the barranca, the Ferris wheel, the Loop-a-Plane, the riderless horse - tell him that he is a frustrated near-hero. All of the above symbols - and more - are the Consul (and to a large extent, Lowry too): a neo-Romantic, a Satanic-Byronic, self dramatizing figure of a man. Passage after passage in the novel illustrates how Lowry uses symbolism "symptomatically to analyze a complex which is part individual, part a consequence of the times." What we see in the novel is a combination of individual and social neuroses, traced through a wide variety of situations.

Atlantis. The Consul thinks that the lost island of Atlantis may have been the original Garden of Eden. He locates it where Mexico is today. The ancients located it under the ocean somewhere west of the Strait of Gibraltar. Geoffrey nevertheless may have come to Mexico originally in search of Eden. (Yvonne places Eden somewhere further north, particularly Canada.)

Blackstone, William. A seventeenth-century "wizard" who came from Cambridge to New England (almost as Lowry had come), whose writings (like Lowry's) were destroyed by a fire similar to the one that destroyed the Consul's "great work" (described in Yvonne's dying vision in Chapter XI). The Consul's last desperate assumption of William Blackstone's name fails to save him from death.

El Bosque. El Bosque, the "magic wood" cantina, is located at the "terminal," literally and figuratively (Chapter VII).

Cock. The fighting cock is a Cabbalistic symbol of death and atonement. For Geoffrey, however, it takes on (Chapter X) its more vulgar connotation (penis), and thus becomes a symbol of his own impotence with Yvonne earlier in the day. Later, it becomes a symbol of his impotence in the face of death: "Sick... half past sick by the cock," an unintended feeble (but prophetic) pun (pp. 287, 352). The cock is also the ritual animal that will announce the end of the Consul's stay on earth that day (cf. The Day of the Dead), his death, and the return of his soul to its proper resting place. And the number 7 again: The Consul also recalls "the strange Indian belief prevailing that a cock would crow over a drowned body...shrilly seven times!" (Chapter XII).

Corpse-Train. As the returning Yvonne approaches the Bella vista bar (Chapter II), she hears Geoffrey say that "a corpse will be transported by express." Her arrival synchronized with that announcement, is symbolic of the Consul's thinly disguised death wish. The corpse is that of a child, and thus symbolizes the total sterility of Geoffrey's love (not Yvonne's sterility, since we learn that she had had a child by her previous marriage). Throughout the day, Yvonne comes to realize that every act Geoffrey performs is intended to kill her (she is love), and in the end he does kill her (love) by releasing the horse that tramples her to death in the dark woods below the Farolito. The Consul has long before realized that "No se puede vivir sin amar" - "It is impossible to live without love" - but he is impotent to do anything about it.

The train can be a bearer of corpses (Geoffrey's original observation); it can also be a bearer of souls to their ultimate destination (Geoffrey's new vision). (Chapter X. See other references: pp. 282–3, 284, 287, 301.)

La Despedida. "...a great rock split by forest fires." The Spanish word also means "The Parting." Yvonne realizes the inevitability of their separation once again. "The violence of the fire which split the rock apart had also incited the destruction of each separate rock, canceling the power that might have held them unities... She longed to heal the cleft rock" (pp. 54-55).

Dogs. Dogs, especially the black pariah dog that insists on following Geoffrey around, may symbolize (a) the satanic black poodle, companion to Goethe's (not Marlowe's) Faust, and (b) abject humility (modesty and earthiness, a quality more indigenous to Mexicans and other underprivileged people than to Anglos), something Geoffrey would like to achieve, but cannot. Geoffrey's day (and life) ends with this humility achieved - the dog is thrown into the barranca with our pathetic "Faust." The starving pariah dog is also the embodiment of the Consul's own thirst (for tequila, for "light," for redemption). Note how the Consul, now confident of his "inevitable" role as messiah, imitates Jesus' own words, saying to the dog, "Yet this day, pichicho, shalt thou be with me in." - The unsaid word is, of course, the barranca, hell (Chapter VII).

The Aztecs always provided a dog with the corpse of the sacrificed god. (Cf. Geoffrey's indirect **allusion** to his "Christliness.") Perhaps, as the Aztecs believed, this black pariah dog will allow Geoffrey's spirit to swim on his (the dog's) back over the water of the dead. And, after a four-year trip, the spirit (and the dog) would arrive before the appropriate god, present his "papers," and then be admitted (with the dog) to the "Ninth Abyss." The Consul is thus presented with an alternative form of "salvation": Should he be denied Christian salvation, he may then still be eligible for Aztec salvation.

Eagle. The national emblem of Mexico is the eagle holding a serpent in its beak. The serpent has all sorts of symbolic meanings, including those associated with the Garden of Eden

(Mexico is Geoffrey's "garden pro tem") seduction, betrayal, etc. When Yvonne releases the caged eagle (Chapter XI), she is freeing Geoffrey (the eagle), and watches the symbol rise into the dark blue sky where she herself is soon to be lifted in death to the stars. By a happy etymological - and literary - coincidence, Quauhnauhuac (the old Indian name for Cuernavaca) is the place "where the eagle stops." And so Yvonne frees the eagle (the Consul's soul), having finally realized Geoffrey's need for freedom (p. 320).

Farolito. When Geoffrey earlier outlines for Yvonne the actual setting for his own death, he notes in triangular fashion the volcano Popocatepetl at the apex, and the barranca and the Farolito directly beneath it at the corresponding base angles (p. 339). We have here, then, not only the Cabbalistic sign for the earth (the triangle), but also the volcano as symbolic of the destruction of earth. (We also have a much-simplified explanation of the book's title.) The Farolito, one of the three key elements above, - "the lighthouse that invited the storm" - symbolizes the central struggle between light and darkness; the paradoxical center where light and darkness meet and merge. The Farolito at Parian may be compared with the Pharos at Alexandria, the lighthouse to which alchemists in ancient times attributed supernatural influences.

Fructuoso Sanabria. Literally translated, the name of the one of the Consul's assassins (Chapter XII) means "Fruitful Saint of the Yawning Path - or Saint of the Abyss." (He is also referred to as Chief of Gardens.) This name is one of the few characteronymics used by Lowry. See also Doctor Vigil, Concepta, Diosdado, and Laruelle.

Garden Of Eden. In Cabbalistic lore, the Garden of Eden is actually a mental construct: God has planted the choice between good and evil in the human mind. The Consul recognizes this in his reference to this garden wherein life is in equipoise between two opposing forces. (Cf. also Iago's "garden" speech in *Othello*, I, iii, 322–337.)

Goat. The goat symbolizes lechery, cuckoldry, and tragedy. The goat that attacks Hugh and Yvonne (Chapter IV) is a triple image: a "tragedy" is literally a "goat song": cabron is the Spanish word for "goat" and also for "cuckold"; also, Azazel, the Hebrew word for "scapegoat."

Golf Ball. The soul is now a golf ball that will eventually go into the "Golgotha Hole." The Consul observes that "It had shown lack of imagination to build the golf course back up there, remote from the barranca. Golf=gouffre=gulf" (p. 202). In Chapter XI, the Consul observes that the make of the golf ball is "Zodiac Zone." We are back to the fatal number 12.

Good Samaritan. The connection between the biblical parable and the Indian left to die by the wayside is made time and time again. The ship that the Consul commanded in World War I was called the Samaritan. The Consul never got over his sense of guilt for having permitted the occupants of the German Q-boat to be consumed in the flames of that ship.

Guitar. Hugh reflects, if he ever came to write his autobiography, "he would have to admit that a guitar made a pretty important symbol in his life" (p. 154). At least for that part of his life devoted to music. The guitar reappears on pp. 305–6, and again on p. 327.

Hell Bunker. Hell is also reminiscent of Hell Bunker (as Laruelle recollects in Chapter I), the place where the Taskerson boys (and guests) took their girls, innocently, of course.

The underground connection between the "innocent" hell of the seaside golf course (Lowry at fifteen was the boy golf champion of all England) and the abyss - the barranca of Malebolge at Quauhnauhuac - serves to point up the Consul's earliest preoccupation with what must be his ultimate destiny. (See "Golf Ball entry above.) It should also help to reinforce the basic symbolic myth of the novel.

Himalayas (Himavat). Earlier, this dream of the Himalayas had been a vision of heaven. In the "bathroom epiphany" (Chapter V) the vision of creation - the new moon with the old one in its arms -symbolizes the Consul's desire to return to his childhood (he was born in the Himalayas), to innocence.

Insect. The insect escaping from the cat (Chapter V) may symbolize the Consul's soul eventually ascending to the top of Popocatepetl on the very last page of the novel, perhaps to join Yvonne's soul in Paradise. Still, we know that the Consul's descent into the barranca is intended to tell us that he is eternally damned to hell. But can he not be saved by the love of a "good" woman? The possible analogy between the Consul (a would-be Christ figure) and Christ should persuade the reader to consider the Consul's eventual redemption.

Locust. The carapace of a seven-year locust appears in Chapter V. Consider this as just another gratuitous reference to the fatal, Cabbalistic number 7.

Loop-The-Loop. The Loop-the-Loop (or Loop-a-Plane) in Chapter VII suggests to Geoffrey that he is Ixion on a wheel eternally turning in hell and slowly destroying the lives caught up in it. The wheel (appropriately called La Maquina Infernal, "the infernal machine") is not to be confused with the Ferris wheel representing Buddha's wheel of law, of eternity.

The Consul, upside down on the wheel as if ready to make his headlong plunge into hell, strikes the children below as very funny. He doesn't think it so funny when all the contents of his pockets fall out and down to the ground, as if his total identity were being taken from him. His passport is missing: did he or did he not have it with him?

Matlalcueyatl. In Chapter X, the Consul briefly considers Matlalcueyatl, rather than Popocatepetl, as the mountain where he will cleanse his soul. The travel folder speaks of this mountain as the place where one will still find "the ruins of the shrine dedicated to the God of Waters, Tlaloc..." The train for Tlaxcala leaves, symbolically, at 7:30 p.m. - a half-hour after his death that day - and arrives at 12:00 a.m. (the magic number 12 again, the 12 stages of initiation or passage to paradise).

But the Consul misses the bus to Tlaxcala. This leads him into a long stream-of-consciousness dissertation on "sacred fire" in which mescal ("honey water" to the Aztecs, the "nectar of immortality" to the Indo-Aryans) becomes "magic fire." "Water" has been turned into "fire"; "fire" will now disclose the truth that will lead him to true salvation.

Mescal. In Parian, mescal, the "illusion of grace," can be obtained (Chapter III). When Yvonne drinks her first mescal at El Popo, she enters for the first time into the Consul's magical-mystical world (Chapter XI). She can now release the "eagle."

Orlac. The next showing of Las Manos de Orlac is scheduled for 6:30 p.m., the approximate time when the Consul will begin his battle against the "murderer's hands" of the fascist police.

"Papa." The only direct reference to Geoffrey as "Papa" occurs on p. 117, where Hugh quotes the doctor as saying about

Geoffrey that "so far as he knew there was nothing wrong with Papa and never had been save that he wouldn't make up his mind to stop drinking." In several other pages of the novel, the reader will come upon the statement, Es inevitable la muerte del Papa, "The Pope's death is inevitable." In actual fact, Pope Pius XI was fatally ill at that time; however, there is no doubt that Geoffrey is also referring to his own inevitable death through that statement.

Pleiades. Many ancient civilizations (including the Aztec) worshipped the Pleiades. By coincidence, perhaps (with the exception of the Mexican Day of the Dead), the Christian holidays of All Hallows (Eve) Day and All Saints Day fall out within the three-day period in which the Pleiades moved out. In her dying vision (Chapter XI) of fire and stars, Yvonne feels herself "suddenly gathered upwards and borne towards the stars...towards Orion, the Pleiades..." Lowry was aware not only of the "coincidental" relationship of Christian holidays with the time of the moving out of the Pleiades, but also of the ancient Mexican custom of placating the gods during that time with a human sacrifice "on whose still living breast a fire of wood was kindled..."

Popocatepetl. To Yvonne, born in Hawaii where volcanoes are rather common, Popocatepetl is a spiritual symbol of home, security, and innocence.

Prometheus. The Consul, like Prometheus, is also a stealer of divine light (mysteries, truth, "fire"), and will similarly experience the punishment of torment.

Quauhnauhuac. Weber, the American fascist agent, delivers a violent tirade against an earlier "revolution" in Quauhnauhuac (p. 99). The description is essentially the same as appeared in many newspapers at that time of the wholesale slaughter of Loyalist sympathizers in the bullring in Guernica.

Quincey. To accommodate his reference to *Macbeth*, the Consul changes the name of his critical neighbor from Quincey to De Quince. He is now ready to refer to Thomas De Quincey's well-known essay. "On the Knocking on the Gate," in which the author explains the significance of that scene in the play. Immediately after Macbeth (and Lady Macbeth) having killed King Duncan, there is a knocking at the gate. It is Macduff, come to see the King. De Quincey (and others) interpret this as the beginning of Macbeth's retribution; Macduff is his nemesis; the gate is now the gate of hell, and Macbeth will very soon begin to pay back for his crime. The play on the word **catastrophe** in this passage (p. 136) adds to that interpretation.

Rabbit. "In one corner of the room sat a white rabbit eating an ear of Indian corn" (p. 337). The rabbit nibbling away at an ear of corn is symbolic of the rabbit that is the Aztec god of drink. It is also a projection of the Consul himself. (Cf. Mary Chase's play, Harvey, in which Harvey is the big white rabbit that only Elwood P. Dowd, the gentle dipsomaniac, can see.) "Everything is to be found in Peter Rabbit," Hugh quotes the Consul as saying (Chapter VI).

Scorpion. Scorpio being the Consul's horoscope sign, "As Scorpio sets in the southwest" -Geoffrey preparing to descend into the abyss - "the Pleiades are rising in the northeast" - Yvonne prepares to rejoin the stars (in death). The action of the novel takes place on November 2, when the zodiac sign is Scorpio. The scorpion is a symbol of suicide; in the garden, the Consul predicts that they "will only sting themselves to death," even as he continues to risk his own life with the death-sting of alcohol.

"St. Louis Blues." The "St. Louis Blues" can be heard near the Ferris wheel. The blues **theme** (and the color blue motif) runs throughout this chapter (VII). It suggests the Consul (the man with the blue eyes) and the ruined blue Ford (the Consul is a habitual wrecker of cars).

Tower Of Babel. The Tower of Babel here (Chapter X) - "a babel of glasses - towering...built to the sky..." - symbolizes the Consul's confusion of identity. What follows is the lengthy catalog of the empty bottles (p. 292).

Wheels. The Consul refers to his "shakes" as "wheels within wheels" (Chapter VI). Compare this image with the vision of Ezekiel, 1:15: "When they went, they went in any of their four directions without turning as they went..." In Chapter VII, the carousel pictures are painted on an "inner wheel." One picture, the wheel of life depicting animal and earthy things, the Garden of Eden, is a kind of Jungian memory trace for Geoffrey.

There are still other "wheels": the roulette wheel (p. 267), the wheel of a boy's bicycle (p. 280), "the sun revolving around the luminous wheel of this galaxy (p. 322), the lottery wheels (p. 329).

Windmill. The poster for Las Manos de Orlac and the toy windmill (Chapter IV) foreshadow the Indian's death; also Hugh's efforts to help him are compared to tilting at windmills.

Yvonne's Blouse. The blouse Yvonne is wearing in Chapter IV is embroidered with birds (Yvonne herself), flowers (fertility promised), and pyramids (triune worlds of the Tree of Life - three-sided).

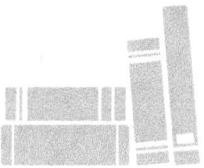

UNDER THE VOLCANO

TEXTUAL ANALYSIS

CHAPTER I

Taskerson. Laruelle reminisces about the visit he and the Consul had made as very young men to the Taskersons. This is the first substantial flashback in the novel (the subsequent eleven chapters will constitute in themselves extended flashbacks). We learn about Geoffrey's youthful days through this flashback. Another Taskerson flashback will occur in Chapter V, in VII (Geoffrey singing the Taskerson song to himself), and in XII, wherein the Consul makes a feeble attempt to walk as upright (when drunk) as he did during the Taskerson stay.

Musical Development. As the plot is being laid out in this chapter, several of the **themes** and counter-themes of the novel are being stated for the first time. Lowry, with his penchant for musical composition, will develop these themes, play variations on them, strike "chords" (for example, the "chord" of Yvonne's death in Chapter XI is first struck here, to be "resolved" later on), and reach the "coda" in the final chapter.

Wheel. The Ferris wheel is to be seen as the Buddha wheel of the law, of eternal, ineluctable recurrence and return. It is the form, structure, skeleton, and dynamic of the novel. In its simplest terms, it can be moved backward - and it does move backward at one point - to recapitulate the events of the past year. The circular ride also suggests movement without progression, eternal recurrence, as well as man's drunken plunge to disaster. After his ride on another wheel, the Consul returns to earth to meet a group of open-mouthed children waiting to return to him all the items that fell out of his pockets when he was upside down on the wheel - everything except his passport (his identity), which he now can't remember having had with him before the ride.

Cinema. Since the reader will be indebted to Laruelle for finding out just what did happen the year before, he can accept the eleven chapters that follow as Laruelle's cinematic creation. The Ferris wheel then becomes of necessity an enormous reel of movie film that will provide him with an instant "replay" of the events of 1938. In this sense, then, this movie reel becomes the wheel of time, turning us back to the year before, to Chapter II and the rest.

Cabbala, Drunkenness, Garden. The Cabbala considers 70 (a multiple of 7, one of three basic numbers, 3 and 12 being the other two) a magical number. It represents the number of elders to whom Moses himself communicated the secret doctrine, the Hebrew word Sod ("secret"), and wine. Since wine was considered by the Cabbalists as the outstanding symbol of creation (cf. also the Dionysian revels celebrating fecundity and birth), the "guarded words that have never been revealed to man," it followed, therefore, that drunkenness would be construed as a misuse of magical powers. (The Aztecs had a similar interpretation of drunkenness.) Lowry appropriates this aspect of the Hebrew word Sod to extend its meaning to a neglected garden, relying on the fact that the Cabbala is sometimes considered as the garden itself, with the Tree of Life (the Tree of the Forbidden Fruit in the Garden of Eden; the forbidden fruit was, of course, grapes, not apples) the centerpiece of that garden.

The "vine" is also a lesser known epithet for God, and Lowry's concept of drunkenness coincides with the Zoharistic construction of Noah's drunkenness as a "blasphemous revelation of divine secrets." He is also indebted to Philo for that excellent example of oxymoron, "sober drunkenness," which appears several times throughout the novel. Philo looked upon man's union with God as sobria inebriatas, sober drunkenness. (In later times, cf. Spinoza, the "God-intoxicated" man.)

Fire. Fire, as embodied in the cantina's candlelight, symbolizes enlightenment. It also symbolizes purification, as when Jacques Laruelle's burning of the Consul's unsent letter to Yvonne ritualistically releases Geoffrey's soul. This "fire" is underscored by the final tolling of the bell, signifying that the Day of the Dead is ended, and that now the dead can return to their eternal resting-place.

This final scene also parallels Yvonne's dying vision (Chapter XI) of the Consul's burning book, and the bells that toll Geoffrey's death (Chapter XII). Outside the cantina, the Ferris wheel (the wheel of life and time) begins to turn backward, and we are now ready to witness the "replay" of the Consul's fatal day twelve months ago.

UNDER THE VOLCANO

TEXTUAL ANALYSIS

CHAPTER II

....

Musical Development. The enigmatic "contrapuntual" dialogue in the Bella Vista bar comes from Weber. Later, he is identified as the smuggler who flew Hugh down to Mexico, and is also involved with the Sinarchistas in the Farolito, when they murder the Consul. The "chord" of No se puede vivir sin amar is stated for the first time in the form of the graffito outside Laruelle's house.

Wheel. The wheel motif in this chapter is represented by the flywheel in the printer's shop.

Cinema. Still another film enjoying a "return engagement" (after nine years) is Las Manos de Orlac, significant in that it parallels the impossible love relationship between the Consul and Yvonne. This film, plus the posters announcing the boxing match in town, points up the hopelessness, of Yvonne's return to the Consul to effect a reconciliation.

Eve's Return. Yvonne is Eve returning to the scene of her lost innocence. She is, as it were, responding to Geoffrey's magical message to her to come back (the letter itself was never sent.) She is returning as "a messenger of light who is both judge and love."

UNDER THE VOLCANO

TEXTUAL ANALYSIS

CHAPTER III

....

Musical Development. By a kind of strained counterpoint, the scene between the impotent Consul and Yvonne in this chapter is balanced by the scene in Chapter XII between the Consul and the whore Maria. The Consul's impotence with Yvonne must be construed as spiritual, as well as psychogenic.

Dead Indian - Major Image. The dead man with sombrero over his eyes that the Consul sees in the garden is the prevision (provided by delirium tremens) of the dead Indian with sombrero over his eyes lying by the wayside in Chapter VIII.

Garden. Geoffrey and Yvonne enter the ruined garden; his contrast of the once-fecund past (when she was present to tend the garden) with the barren present (the garden overgrown and untended by him since their divorce) continues the sterility **theme** (cf. the rotten egg and the funeral of the dead child in the preceding chapter).

Telephone. The telephone rings, and one of the several significantly confused conversations begins. The caller is trying to warn Geoffrey that his position in Mexico is now very precarious (undefended since he is no longer the British consul in Cuernavaca), and that he ought to leave the country while he can. Geoffrey is annoyed, and hangs up the receiver the wrong way. If Lowry is depicting in this way another attempt at communication "from above," then the Consul is already determined to reject any supernatural - as well as human - warnings or assistance.

Geoffrey's position is indeed precarious; as precarious as that of a diplomatic college of his in Tlaxcala, whose property has been confiscated. But he won't leave Mexico; instead, he may become a Mexican subject; better still, he will go to live among the Indians, as William Blackstone did. (No use: his pretending to be Blackstone doesn't save him from the assassins in Chapter XII.) But even as he rejects Yvonne's suggestion to leave Mexico with her, he realizes for the first time that he is adumbrating his coming martyrdom - and salvation. He also experiences for the first time the phenomenon described by Philo as a mystical sobria inebriata ("sober drunkenness).

UNDER THE VOLCANO

TEXTUAL ANALYSIS

CHAPTER IV

....

Musical Development. The "chord" of the dead-Indian-to-be (Chapter VIII) and the "chord" of Yvonne's death (Chapter XI) are sounded here: the dead-Indian-to-be first appears outside the cantina La Sepultura (The Tomb) with his horse (the one that a crazed and confused Consul will accidentally release to kill Yvonne) tied up nearby. The "countermovement" to this double chord is the Battle of the Ebro, being lost at that very same time in the Spanish Civil War. Elsewhere in the Consul's finite cosmos, nobody seems to care enough to do anything about the imminent death of the Spanish Republic, just as in Mexico nobody seems to care to do anything (except rob him) about the Indian dying by the wayside.

Day Of The Dead. On this one day of the year, the belief is that the dead come to life for one day. With Yvonne's return on this day, Geoffrey will once again be brought back to life (by her love), only that he may die again. Yvonne will also motivate Hugh to seek for selflessness in dying and being reborn at sea (the source of all life). Two brothers will thus die, but in effect one half will die for the other half in that Hugh is but another persona of Geoffrey, an extension. (The biological fact that Hugh is Geoffrey's half-brother may or may not be considered in this instance; the decision is left to the reader.)

UNDER THE VOLCANO

TEXTUAL ANALYSIS

CHAPTER V

....

Musical Development. Chapter IV closed with the words: "It was as though he were gazing now beyond this expanse of plains and beyond the volcanoes out to the wide rolling blue ocean itself...," words of liberation, release, freedom. The opening of Chapter V comments ironically on those words: "Behind them walked the only living thing that shared their pilgrimage, the dog. And by degrees they reached the briny sea..." The quasi-musical bridge thus constructed indicates how the action is now moving quickly out of the realm of the physical and into the realm of the mind. The Consul will, of course, never reach "the briny sea," (or liberation), the beginnings of all life. The dog (like the one that will be thrown into the barranca with the dying Consul) may be "the only living thing" to share their (Hugh's and Yvonne's) pilgrimage, but it also symbolizes the Consul's inevitable death.

Garden. The most important **theme** of the book is now stated for the first time: Le Gusta Este Jardin? Que Es Suyo? Evite Que Sus Hijos Lo Destruyan! "Do you like this garden..." The Consul mistranslates the sign. The garden is the Garden of Eden, and it could be God himself, rather than the civic-minded local authorities, who could be asking the question. (Actually the sign says that if you like this garden, try to keep your children from destroying it.) The garden is also the world. Use it (the garden or the world) badly, and, like Adam and Eve, you too will be dispossessed from it.

Himalayas. Geoffrey's dream-nightmare-meditation at the opening of this chapter represents his spirit climbing upward into the Himalayas (the Consul was born in Kashmir) in seven degrees. The dream occurs simultaneously with Hugh's ride (Chapter IV), thereby **foreshadowing** Hugh's wish to climb Popocatepetl later on and the Consul's dying vision. Lowry in effect is providing the Consul with the clairvoyance, prevision, and premonition that the Consul ascribes to magical powers.

Bathroom Epiphanies. Why the "bathroom meditation"? Hugh had expressed a strong desire to climb Popocatepetl (cf. Geoffrey's dream of climbing the Himalayas earlier); Geoffrey now considers the possibility of descending into the barranca "...to visit the cloacal Prometheus who doubtless inhabited it." (Italics added) There will be two other such bathroom or cloacal (literally, of the sewer or cesspool) "epiphanies" later on. In this first "epiphany," the Consul for the first time debates with himself his ability and/or obligation to assume the guilt of the world on his own unreliable shoulders. Is he really the one to perform the messianic descent into the barranca? The bathroom or "jakes" or "john" (Revelation According to St. John?) as a suitable setting for such a profound observation may recall the ancient earthy saying: "Inter urinam et feces nascimur."

UNDER THE VOLCANO

TEXTUAL ANALYSIS

CHAPTER VI

....

Guilt Motif. We are now at the midpoint of the novel, at the midpoint of life, at the "heart" of the book. The central character in this chapter is Hugh, twenty-nine years old, the Consul's younger self (the Consul is forty-one). The **theme** of the Inferno is restated in the slightly garbled opening lines of Dante's *Inferno*: "In the middle of our life, etc..." Hugh expresses his own - and Everyman's - guilt for things done, for things that should have been done. He is the "youth of Everyman," so full of ambitions and aspirations, richly endowed with talents still to be used. He is also middle-aged Everyman, full of frustrations and failings - the poet, musician, seaman, composer he never really became. He wanted to be accepted at sea, as part of the "brotherhood of man," to act the Good Samaritan. But the "cut" to the picture of the Samaritan is a reminder that in Chapter VIII Geoffrey will fail the Indian dying by the wayside, and that in Chapter XII Hugh will fail the dying Geoffrey (and helpless Geoffrey will fail the dying Yvonne). Hugh's frustrations make him out to be only a slightly lesser dipsomaniac than his brother.

Stylistically, Hugh's meditation counterbalances Geoffrey's earlier "bathroom epiphany." The two half brothers (or the two halves of the one person) are thus tied together through the complementary rituals.

UNDER THE VOLCANO

TEXTUAL ANALYSIS

CHAPTER VII

....

Numerology. This chapter could well have been titled "The Consul's Last Chance." The sense of doom is all too palpable. Es inevitable la muerte del Papa translates literally as "The death of the Pope is inevitable," or more freely, "The Consul must die."

The Consul must die because (as Lowry would argue numerologically) "his number is up," and the number happens to be 7. The horseman of Chapter IV, who is to be the Indian dying on the roadside in Chapter VIII, rides a horse with the number 7 branded on his rump. This same horse will kill Yvonne in Chapter XI. Furthermore, the Consul will die promptly at 7 p.m. And, not unexpectedly, the chapter of doom is Chapter VII.

Mexican folklore includes an elaborate seven-day journey to be taken by the souls of the newly dead. The journey also involves a trial descent into the darkness of the abyss. The Consul's journey into hell covers the time period from 7 a.m. to 7 p.m. The Consul welcomes back Yvonne at 7 a.m. on November 2, 1938.

The number 7 likewise refers to the number of heavenly palaces and tower steps to heaven or to hell. There are seven ledges of purgatory. The number 7 also represents the Pleiades, and a traditional biblical number designating sacrifice. Adam was given Eve on the seventh day. And on the seventh day, God rested. That is, He left mankind to his own devices. Or, in another sense, abandoned him.

(Lowry personally considered the number 7 magical, both in a good and bad sense. He moved into his Cuernavaca apartment house on January 7. His house in Canada burned down on June 7, 1944. When he returned to the burned-down site, he found that someone had branded the number 7 on a burned tree.)

Messiah. The Consul is now discovering still other "confirmations" of his messianic role (first "revealed" to him in the bathroom in Chapter V). In the Farolito, he recalls in particular one incident in which "...the beggars...one of whom one night...had taken him for the Christ, and falling down on his knees before him, had pinned...two medallions... portraying the Virgin of Guadalupe...on him." It could have been brought about by the Consul's beard, or the surroundings, or the recollection that on the Day of the Dead, many Mexicans crawl on their knees up the steps leading to shrines dedicated to Our Lady of Guadalupe. And in Mexico anything is possible, even an "alcoholic Christ." And after the Day of the Dead has ended, the anticipated calm will come to him. He impatiently checks the time to ascertain how soon he will be able to make the final, noble gesture, for "nothing in his life so became him as the leaving it."

UNDER THE VOLCANO

TEXTUAL ANALYSIS

CHAPTER VIII

"Downhill." The first word of the chapter, "Downhill," indicates that the action is moving toward the abyss, toward the climax.

The Indian on the horse branded number 7 now appears in the most crucial incident in the novel. In Chapter IV, he had been sitting outside the pulqueria. In Chapter VII, he had appeared singing. Now he is dying by the wayside, his fateful horse nearby.

Memento Mori. The Indian can be taken to symbolize mankind itself, mankind dying specifically in the critical battle of the Spanish Civil War, the Battle of the Ebro in 1938, or now (World War II) in Europe. The rest of us do nothing about this but talk, like the Consul himself, confronted with the Indian dying by the wayside. The Indian is also, in a sense, the Consul himself (the Consul has already identified himself with the Indian in Chapter VII). From Chapter I on, the Indian has figured as the Consul's shadow, the shadow of death, the Consul's own memento mori.

The seminal **theme** of the dying Indian is also intended to point up some very significant moral and political implications. The Indian symbolizes the rape and murder of Mexico being committed by the fascists; a replay, as it were, of the Spanish Conquest, the attempted conquest by Maximilian, and the exploitation of Mexico's natural resources by the Anglo-Saxon powers. It is indicative of the Consul's apolitical posture that he doesn't seem to remember that he is an ex-consul, subject to immediate eviction, because Mexico's recent nationalization of its oil wells had precipitated the break in diplomatic relations between that country and Great Britain.

Vultures. The xopilotes or vultures are real and indigenous to Mexico. They fly throughout the novel, angels of death in this land where the people (to reverse Coleridge's phrase) lead a death-in-life existence. In Chapter XI, the vultures become (according to Lowry) "as it were archetypal Promethean fowl." In the city of Tula, a Toltec pyramid dedicated to Quetzalcoatl depicts eagles and vultures eating bleeding hearts. In Greek mythology, as we know, the vultures eat away at Prometheus' liver. When Lowry refers to the vultures as "Promethean fowl," he is responsible, perhaps unintentionally, for a clinical commentary on cirrhosis, the effect of excessive drinking on the liver.

Telephone Poles. As in Chapter III, the telephone poles symbolize the lack of communication among the characters themselves, and between the Consul and his supernatural "correspondents." The radio is never static-free, apparently because somebody (or something) down here doesn't want him to receive the life-saving messages from somebody (or something) up there.

UNDER THE VOLCANO

TEXTUAL ANALYSIS

CHAPTER IX

....

Musical Development. The chapter as originally written represented Hugh's point of view; its first rewriting represented the Consul's point of view; as it now stands (in its second rewriting), it represents Yvonne's point of view. Lowry considered this chapter to be, in a musical sense, a fine contrast to Chapter VIII and Chapter X. The threads of the various **themes** of the novel begin to come together in anticipation of the "coda" of this strange "symphony."

Flashbacks. Since the main point of this chapter is hope, the flashbacks serve to emphasize the novel's vacillations between past and future, between despair (the past) and hope (the future); between sending the Consul to Guanajuato and rebirth, or to Parian and extinction.

Past As Burden. At the end of the chapter, the image of the Indian carrying his father represents the restated, universalized **theme** of mankind struggling helplessly under the "eternal tragic weight of the past." The image is also Freudian, Oedipean ("man eternally carrying the psychological burden of his father," the sense of guilt for having killed - or unconsciously wishing to kill - his father). The image also serves once again to relate the Indian to the Consul.

Bullfight. For Yvonne the "moment of truth" in the arena does not have to be the moment when the coup de grace is administered to the bull. It comes when, seeing the ineptness of the drunken Mexicans trying to lasso the bull, she immediately equates that with the ineptness with which Geoffrey has handled his own life. For her the bull-throwing **episode** becomes an extended **metaphor** of life, death, and resurrection; in another context, it becomes an extended **metaphor** of the failures of the men in her life - Cliff Wright, Geoffrey, Laruelle, Hugh, and, of course, her own father.

UNDER THE VOLCANO

TEXTUAL ANALYSIS

CHAPTER X

....

Themes. At the beginning of Chapter II, the cryptic statement "A corpse will be transported by express" appears. This statement, reinforced by the author's own affirmation of the importance of Freudian elements in the novel, is now clarified to some extent by the opening train **theme** in this chapter. The **theme** is related to Freudian death dreams, and the reader can now logically conjecture that the Consul's indecision, despair, and helplessness in the face of recurrent opportunities to save himself is the familiar Freudian "death wish."

The passage on the "Virgin for those who have nobody with" carries the reader back to Chapter I and Doctor Vigil's pseudo-theological discussion with Laruelle.

Tlaxcala. The Tlaxcala folder section is no mere aping of Joyce's "cataloguing" device in Ulysses. If the section had been set up in a variety of type faces (like some of the **Metaphysical** poetry that Lowry knew so well?), it could very well have symbolized the Consul's state of delirium (Lowry's own suggestion).

Tlaxcala, like Parian, symbolizes death. The Tlaxcalans were also considered traitors to Mexico, a historical fact that Lowry uses to symbolize the Consul's surrender to the forces within himself that are betraying - and have already betrayed-him. The section constitutes in itself the phantasmagoria brought on by the Consul's D. T.'s. The dialogue now directs itself more obviously to the **theme** of war (the volcanoes at the close of the chapter now seem closer, and so does the war they symbolize), and also to the Consul's self-destruction.

Bathroom Epiphany. The Tlaxcala travel folder that Geoffrey reads in the bathroom brings on another "epiphany," as well as a substantial infusion of black-magic ambiance. (Tlaxcala was reputed to be the center of black magic in Mexico.) The familiar motifs of train, volcano, and Virgin are now repeated. The Consul now also begins drinking mescal (the sacramental liquor that he once feared) in dead earnest, the final defiance of divine law that will result in his death. Geoffrey bathes his soul in drink (can he thus regain his lost innocence?), even as Hugh and Yvonne try to regain their lost innocence by bathing a second time that day, in the Salon Ofelia pool.

UNDER THE VOLCANO

TEXTUAL ANALYSIS

CHAPTER XI

....

Wheel. In Chapter I the wheel (Ferris wheel or the Buddha wheel) was used to relate the novel to eternity. In this chapter, the wheel comprises the motion of the stars and constellations as they move or spin through the universe. This wheel, too, is used to relate the novel to eternity.

Dante. Dante's wood appears again, this time not as part of a quotation (opening lines of Chapter VI), and not just in the name of a cantina (Casino de la Selva, El Bosque) but as an actual dark wood. The reference to the stars may also be related to the closing lines of Dante's *Paradiso*: "...But like to a wheel whose circling nothing jars/Already on my desire and will prevailed/ The love that moves the sun and the other stars" (Italics added).

Day Of The Dead. The **theme** of the Day of the Dead reappears now with the scene in the cemetery balancing the scene of the mourners in Chapter I.

Eleusinian Mysteries. Yvonne and Hugh go in search of Geoffrey. They pass the wrecks of American cars in the barranca, in particular the one blue abandoned Ford referred to in Chapter I. Events are now coming full circle (cf. the Ferris wheel turning backward in Chapter I); Yvonne is now looking for the Consul, even as much earlier he had been looking for her. Yvonne will not desert Geoffrey again, if she can help it, and if he wishes to be saved by her.

From the close of Chapter X to the close of the book, Lowry uses elements from the Eleusinian Mysteries and the tarot cards (earlier in Chapter VII), along with Cabbalistic elements. The lottery (another wheel?) and the detailed menu (alluded to earlier in Chapter X) comprise a symbolic chart outlining the Eleusinian mystery of the feast-fertility rite. In effect, Yvonne and Hugh may be doing more than searching for the Consul.

Dante And Faust. Yvonne's dying visions are a "replay" of her first thoughts back in Chapters II and IX. At the end of the chapter, she imagines herself being gathered up to the stars (cf. again quotation from Dante's *Paradiso*). She is also Marguerite in the Faust legend. Purified and pardoned, she is lifted up to heaven; beyond absolution or redemption, the Consul/Faust is dragged down to hell by Mephistopheles. Yvonne's imagined celestial trip carries her up through the stars to the Pleiades (of which there are 7; cf. the 7 on the rump of the horse that kills Yvonne, the horse last heard of in Chapter X, that also appeared riderless in Chapter IV, during Yvonne's and Hugh's ride outside La Sepultura). At the same time, the Consul is being thrown directly into the abyss (hell).

Musical Development. All the "chords" previously struck have now been "resolved" in this chapter.

UNDER THE VOLCANO

TEXTUAL ANALYSIS

CHAPTER XII

....

Witches' Sabbath. Appropriately enough, the final chapter is a jumble of symbols, motifs, and themes, some old, some new. The reader is now confronted with a cosmic day-nightmare, a veritable Symphony Fantastique (cf. Lowry's affinity for music), a Walpurgisnacht (cf. Goethe's Faust).

The three-part Witches' Sabbath encompasses three major events, or panels out of a most terrifying tryptich by Hieronymus Bosch:

1. an orgy of drinking and eating

2. sexual intercourse with "an evil succubus in the shape of a woman"

3. human sacrifice and the breaking of the "magic spell," announced by the crowing of the cock.

Blessings, curses, accusations, warnings - all come through in the form of speeches, inner monologues, and the public "desecration" of Yvonne's recovered letters. The epilogue at the close informs us that our latter-day "Christ" has suffered his "Garden of Gethsemane," his "Crucifixion," his "harrowing of Hell" (cf. Easter Saturday), and is finally "risen" (Popocatepetl).

Wheel. Death (as represented by the Farolito in Parian) has finally succeeded in bringing together all the variegated **themes** of the novel - political, esoteric, tragicomical, religious, magical, psychological, etc. The "wheel," though it was moving backward, has nonetheless come full circle: the wheel "whose circling nothing jars."

The Novel As Cathedral. If Chapter I was the westerly tower of the Churrigueresque Mexican cathedral (Lowry said), then Chapter XII is the easterly tower. (Churrigueresque - after the Spanish architect, Churriguera, 1665–1725, whose naive type of mission and church architecture, modified by a lack of trained workmen, figured so prominently in Spanish colonial buildings.) The gargoyles of the westerly tower are repeated in the gargoyles of the easterly tower. The doleful bells of one tower echo the dolefull bells of the other tower. The hopeless letters of Yvonne found by the Consul in this chapter provide a counterpoint (architectonically, if not musically) to the hopeless, unmailed letter of the Consul to Yvonne found by Laruelle a year later in Chapter I. The "slightly ridiculous horse" first mentioned in Chapter I has come full gallop (after at least fifteen citations earlier) in this chapter. The Consul releases the horse, and in so doing, releases the powers of evil that eventually kill Yvonne.

Humor. The novel is neither high tragedy nor low comedy. Lowry's naturally comic bent (more ironic than Falstaffian; the puns rival Eliot's ironic puns) provides a bridge between the naturalistic and the transcendental, and back to the naturalistic. The Consul (and Lowry) is apparently uncomfortable in the face of stark tragedy; hence the humor.

    Cinema. Depending on the director or cutter, the internal basic use of time in a film "depends on the speed at which one scene moves and on the amount of footage devoted to another." Lowry drew upon his experiences in Hollywood to decide finally whether he wanted moving characters against a static background, or static (or near-static) characters against a dynamic background. Since this is Mexico, an innately violent country, he opted for the latter. Then, more in the role of editor and cutter, rather than director, he arranged his sequences after they had been "filmed" in the most dramatically - and, fortunately, novelistically too - efficacious way. It is impossible to know at this time whether Lowry had contemplated an eventual screen adaptation of this novel; there is no doubt, on the other hand, that he was writing a screen scenario at the same time that he was writing a novel. The reader is confirmed in this assumption in Lowry's own suggestion that the book should be construed as "essentially trochal [like a wheel], I repeat, the form of it as a wheel so that, when you get to the end, if you have read carefully, you should want to turn back to the beginning again…"

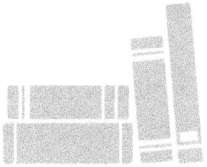

UNDER THE VOLCANO

CHARACTERIZATION

To understand the characters in *Under the Volcano*, one should remember first that Lowry in his brief forty-eight years had been a sailor, song writer, better-than-average athlete, movie scenario writer, poet, and pioneer in Vancouver. For example, much of Hugh's long interior monologue (pp. 154–73) covers Lowry's pre-Mexican years, his experiences at sea (first reported in *Ultramarine*), and his several efforts at song-writing. Also, that since Lowry believed that every man was really two men in one (Hugh is both half-brother to Geoffrey and also the other half of Geoffrey), that is, that every man had a double or doppleganger, he as omnipresent author would appear in almost every one of these roles in the novel itself. Lowry made no effort "to maintain a figurative distance between author, work, and reader,...resisting every effort at literal interpretation" (William Gass). He felt that without the double or doppleganger, the pitiable state of man could neither be clarified nor understood. Consequently, the reader should expect the Consul to have several doubles who at every point in the novel reflect his own helplessness and doom.

Consul As Addict. Lowry says that for Geoffrey Firmin "life is always just around the corner, in the form of another drink at a new bar" (p. 341). He is also probably the first fictional character to "reflect fully the noblesse oblige of the addict, the kind of pride that must be asserted to seek in drink a means of transcending the agony of consciousness" (Richard Costa).

The Consul is charitably characterized as a tragic, addictive Faust in Chapters I and II, and admiringly characterized as a Falstaff in Chapters III and V. He is, in short, a tragicomic figure, not a hero, not even a picaro. He doesn't have the overpowering mentality of a Faust (he - or Lowry - does have Faust's affinity for magic), nor does he have Falstaff's "redeeming" ability to hold his liquor. As for his-so called comic talents, he is as funny as the naive characters who become the "life of the party" after a few drinks.

In Chapter V, the Garden chapter, the Consul becomes confused between his role as Falstaff and his role as Adam. In searching for his "bottle of sack" (the bottle of tequila which he had hidden there three days earlier), he notices the sign nearby: Le Gusta Este Jardin?/Que Es Suyo?/Evite Que Sus Hijos Lo Destruyan! His heretofore adequate knowledge of Spanish causes him to mistranslate the message. But there is enough fidelity to the original to convey the message both to him and to the reader: "If you like this garden, don't destroy it, or you will be evicted from it." So he is Adam now (not Faust, not Falstaff) being warned that if he continues to drink (i.e., eats of the "forbidden fruit," actually grapes, not apples) he will be evicted. The "garden" is of course the Garden of Eden and also the world, and he will be dispossessed from the world if he fails to give and receive love. To his neighbor, Mr. Quincey, however, he jestingly suggests that "the original sin was to be an owner of property."

Geoffrey Firmin's negative capability, that is, the quality of knowing what must be done and not being able to do it (for all sorts of reasons), has been compared with that of Billy Budd. Melville, however, has given Billy a convenient out: his stammering literally and spiritually prevents him from speaking out the truth and thus saving himself from the gallows. The Consul, on the contrary, is not impeded from saving himself (by himself or with the help of Yvonne, Hugh, and Laruelle) by his chronic state of drunkenness (he is drunk three-fourths of the time). He flatly rejects all proffers of help; he rejects all possible human options; his sensibility (often heightened, paradoxically, by his frequent intakes of mescal) tells him what is good and what is evil; he knows the world, and chooses to drop out of it. He has opted (whatever the harmful consequences may be) to battle for the survival of consciousness, for the preservation of his own identity. He is not at all interested in "a sober and non-alcoholic Paradise." He has already chosen between the illusion of Paradise and the ultimate reality of life under the volcano - addiction, death, and destruction. "Under the volcano!" he muses. "It was not for nothing the ancients had placed Tartarus under Mount Aetna, nor within it, the monster Typhoeus, with his hundred heads and - relatively - fearful eyes and voices" (p. 339). At the very end, even as he is lying mortally wounded in the barranca, he is certain that his soul will survive, that it will ascend to the very summit of the volcano. It is as though at the very last moment he has composed a new version of the hymn "I Know That My Redeemer Liveth," without acknowledging a kind of death-bed return to the conventional religiosity of his parents.

Consul As Prometheus. The Consul refers to himself as a Prometheus, a thief of the sacred fire (mescal). He is Promethean, not in the broader sense of being daringly original or creative, but in the more mythic sense of being fallen, bound in chains, being slowly chewed to death by vultures real and imagined (cf. the vultures chewing away at the first Prometheus' liver, and the alcohol that is cirrhotically eating away the Consul's liver), alienated from life, unable to love, and in his inability to love paradoxically defining what love is. The Consul is, in short, a Promethean hero for having stolen "fire"; for his "meaningless muddled ideas," some of them the direct result of having imbibed some of this stolen "fire" (he obviously mistook it for "light" or "brightness"), he must spend the rest of his life having his "liver" eaten away by vultures, a situation easily come by in Mexico, where the vultures are indigenous to the country.

Consul As Messiah. Geoffrey Firmin, in his Christ-aspiring role, takes over the dinner (Chapter X), refers to it as "the supper at Emmaus," and, in the words of a soon-to-be-betrayed Christ, says, "What about it, Hugh - do you want to wait for the fish that dies?" The Greek word for fish is Ichthus, an acronym for Jesus Christ, Son of God, Savior, and used by the early secret Christians as their logos or logotype (not the cross).

This brings up a quasi-religious aspect of the Consul - if not of Lowry himself - that caused Aiken to conclude that when Lowry "really wished for the unconscious - the womb, if you will..." he was actually promulgating the Christian concept that one must die in order to be born again. This, of course, is non-Freudian. Another critic has argued that Lowry never wanted to be born at all. "Nor did it strike me as any less than an unexpected and useful compliment that Phillipson, the artist, should have troubled to represent me," the Consul tells Hugh, "... as an immense guitar, inside which an oddly familiar infant was hiding, curled up, as in a womb" (p. 117). This may be Freudian.

But to pursue the theological line a little farther, there is no doubt that the Consul definitely possessed a martyr or messiah complex. His great battle (in which drink was his most indispensable ally) was against death, was a battle "for the survival of the human consciousness," was his heroic effort to die to atone for man's inhumanity to man, to become, as it were, the archetypal Good Samaritan. The Consul is frequently categorized as a bit of a magician, a magus (sorcerer). The Three Magi "adored" (discovered) the Christ child by following the stars. The Christ child grew up to become a magus himself, a "magician," a healer. The mature Christ was tried (as was the Consul, perfunctorily, of course, by the fascist police before they threw him into the barranca to die), crucified, spent a "season" in Hell (Easter Saturday), and rose, reborn.

The Consul, reborn, ascends to Popocatepetl, and thus becomes "the Christ of the Sierra Madre," in competition, so to speak, with "The Christ of the Andes," that towering figure on a mountain top over in South America. (The reader may wish to add this bit of **imagery** to Lowry's affinity for twos, as discussed elsewhere in this Note.) And so the Consul (or Lowry), or any other "outsider," brings a new kind of faith to the poor, benighted pagans at the expense of his own life. Earlier, to be sure, the Spaniards had also brought the "true religion" to Mexico. It is evident from all this that Lowry, however much he denied and rejected his own Wesleyan upbringing, still retained enough of fundamentalist Calvinism (in his unconscious, of course) to attempt to disseminate the "truth." One marvels at the arrogance of a Protestant trying to succeed where the Catholics apparently failed. In Mexico, therefore, there was a Methodism to his (the Consul's) madness.

Consul As Pelado. The Consul in his time has been a "mute, stricken pariah"; he has also been a pelado, a man who has stripped life of its very basic meaning. In short, whether as Hugh, Laruelle, the poor Indian, or the two-hatted pelado,

Geoffrey Firmin is a doomed man. Given choices to make, "he either abnegates his option or chooses by default." Ironically, he lacks the "nerve of success."

Hugh As Redeemer. Hugh Firmin at twenty-nine considers himself midway along life's journey (an obviously Dantean, not modern, middle age). He takes inventory of himself and recalls all his near-misses, his near-achievements - musician and composer, sailor, student, womanizer and adulterer. He is most sensitive, however, about his ineffectual participation in the fight against fascism, and decides that he will make a positive gesture to atone for such former indifference by sailing later in the month from Vera Cruz (the "True Cross," redemption?) with a shipload of dynamite for the Spanish Loyalists.

If Laruelle represents the artistic conscience of the novel, Hugh represents the political conscience. If Geoffrey experiences a psychological, **metaphysical**, and universal guilt for man's general inhumanity to man, Hugh suffers (and speaks) for the political guilt of non-involvement of the 1930s. Considering that it was England that led the forces of appeasement (and the U.S. that led the forces of non-intervention), it is most interesting that an Englishman, Hugh (read Lowry), sounds the mea culpa for Spain being won by the Fascists by default, for China being raped by the Japanese, and for Mexico being debauched by her native fascists, the Sinarchistas.

Hugh As Geoffrey's Judas. Hugh also considers himself Geoffrey's Judas - Cervantes explains that the song, "Black Flowers," says, "I suffer, because your lips say only lies and they have death in a kiss" (p. 306) - because he covets (and may have at one time possessed) Yvonne. The Consul chooses to observe at this time (among other things) that in Taxila, in India, "the widow of a childless man might contract a Levirate marriage with her brother-in-law" (p. 307). The basis for such an unfavorable self-image may be more logically seen in the fact that Hugh came down to Quauhnauhuac (Cuernavaca) with the American fascist, Weber. As we learn later, Weber has been abetting the activities of the Union Militar, the fascist Mexican secret police who eventually murder the Consul. The Consul, in short, very probably dies in place of Hugh.

Hugh is also indirectly responsible for the Consul's death in that he has placed the incriminating telegram about the "headcoming antisemitic campaign" in Geoffrey's coat pocket (Chapter IV). It is this telegram when later found in the Consul's jacket - and now the Consul is wearing his own jacket - that leads to his misidentification by the police. The Consul, as a Cabbalist, is also ipso facto identified with being pro-Jewish. Once again we have here yet another example of the miscommunication throughout the day that eventually contributes to the Consul's death.

Hugh is in constant competition with Geoffrey for the Christ role. He wants to go back to sea (to replay Geoffrey's role on the Samaritan, but this time to spare the German officers). He'll sail from Vera Cruz (the "true Cross") and perhaps stop off at Trinidad (the "Trinity"). If he ever got to write his autobiography, Hugh observes, "he would have to admit that a guitar made a pretty important symbol in his life" (p. 154). His life? The Consul had told Hugh about the artist who wanted to represent him, the Consul, "...as an immense guitar, inside which an oddly familiar infant was hiding, curled up, as in a womb" (p. 177). Whose guitar? Hugh's or the Consul's? In the midst of their search for Geoffrey, Hugh tells Yvonne about the man he met who wanted to sell him a guitar (p. 327). Hugh bought it, if only to have a guitar of his own, for a change. "What do you want a guitar for," Yvonne asks him. "Are you going to play the Internationale or something on it, on board your ship?" (p. 327). The rivalry between Hugh and Geoffrey is more than a conventional sibling rivalry.

Onward, Eternal Youth...Hugh is the world's kid brother. He joins Geoffrey and Yvonne on their trip to Tomalin. At the arena, he jumps into the ring and overpowers the bull (life), while Geoffrey alternately disapproves and scoffs. Hugh is in love with Yvonne, and like Laruelle, has made love to Yvonne, and not always literally behind his brother's back. Hugh chooses to share both, his brother's guitar and his wife. Hugh gets drunk (not quite as drunk as Geoffrey can get drunk), and goes off to sing revolutionary songs in a dark forest (in the company of Yvonne), unaware that at the very same time his brother, or other self, is being assassinated by the fascist police.

The Hughs of this world need more than youth, vigor, verve, and political idealism, Lowry asserts, to avert disaster, theirs and anybody else's.

Brother to Brother. Both Geoffrey and Hugh look toward the East for ultimate truth, guidance, and salvation. Geoffrey longs for the more unworldly India, to Buddha, to Zen, to mysticism; Hugh looks toward the future worker's "paradise," Red China. The "East" is also dawn, a new day, the orient (lower-case o, please) meaning rising or birth, Mecca, Jerusalem. In Shakespeare's King Lear, the comatose king is borne on a litter to Dover (on the east coast of England) to safety, to resuscitation and "resurrection"; the blinded Gloucester is left by Cornwall and Regan to "smell" his way to Dover, the old man plaintively asking any and all, "Knowest thou the way to Dover?" Dover symbolizes this East, safety, death as freedom from suffering for Gloucester.

Three "Faces" of Yvonne. Yvonne is probably a fusion of Lowry's two wives, both would-be writers and failed actresses, especially Jan, the first wife. The Yvonne married to the Consul, Yvonne Firmin, can never distinguish herself completely from the Yvonne Constable, the unmarried daughter of the highly unsuccessful Captain Constable, or from Yvonne Griffaton, the fairly successful Hollywood actress.

The Consul's psychological impotence, his inability to "make it" with Yvonne, may originate in her ambiguous status as daughter-sweetheart(of another)-become-wife. The injunction against incest, albeit operating only in his unconscious, is enough to "castrate" the Consul. (He has no sexual difficulties whatsoever with the whore Maria in Chapter XII.) By the same token, Yvonne's inhibited or qualified love for the Consul may also be explained in Oedipal terms. Yvonne significantly recalls her former lovers, and in particular "her one true love who had committed suicide, her father" (p. 226).

At the Arena Tomalin, Yvonne thinks about her father, who, like Geoffrey, had also been a consul (American representative in Chile), an alcoholic, a luckless investor in many business enterprises in Hawaii and the States. This reminiscence is to be analyzed on several levels. First, it is a throwback to the original short-story version of *Under the Volcano*, where Yvonne is the daughter of the Consul, and Hugh is her fiance. Secondly, if the reminiscence is to be taken as completely unrelated to its literary prototype, then one can say that Yvonne was attracted to Geoffrey because he was so much like her own father. Thirdly, there is the further possibility that the Geoffrey-father nexus was so strongly imbedded in Lowry's subconscious that Lowry was suggesting to the reader that the Consul's impotence, his inability to achieve compatibility with Yvonne on any level was attributable to the Consul's unconscious fear of incest.

Yvonne as "Love Goddess." Yvonne was once a child movie star, an extremely competent equestrienne (she performed her own stunts in films), a natural beauty. Now she is a stricken love goddess, desired by Geoffrey, Hugh, and Laruelle, but (spiritually) unpossessible to all three because of the imperfectibility of love. No se puede vivir sin amar - Life is impossible without love - one of the main mottoes of the novel proclaims. But for Yvonne - and for many others - true love is to be found only on the silver screen, in the magic land of the movies.

Yvonne as "Beatrice." Why Yvonne left Geoffrey is clearly explained within the first few pages of Chapter II. Why she returned to him and why she tried to effect a reconciliation is left to the reader to answer. Is it the eternal myth of the "lost" man saved and redeemed through the love of a "good" woman? A Beatrice redeeming a Dante? Corny as it may sound, that is exactly what the novel concludes after the last page has been completed.

Perhaps, Yvonne thinks, if they could get away from hellish Mexico to the more moderate, "civilized" Vancouver, Geoffrey might find the will to give up drinking and get down to sober, serious work. (The reader can find a version of this "happy ending" in Lowry's *October Ferry to Gabriola*.) The Consul, who had hoped and dreamed of her return (consider the beautifully sincere and passionate letter he wrote and never mailed to her), receives her gladly, tries to make love to her, and fails: "...the sunlight...falling in a single golden line as if in the act of conceiving a God, falling like a lance straight into a block of ice -" (P. 90).

Soon after, the Consul drags Yvonne and Hugh to Parian. There, the Consul, full of alcohol and mescal, is shot at 7 p.m. by the secret fascist police. Yvonne is killed by a frightened horse (expert horsewoman - dramatic irony!) stupidly untied by the Consul. Hugh, drunk and "awash" in a dark forest, cannot help either one. Yvonne is killed because, as one critic has said, "the Consul has wilfully separated himself from her, thereby releasing the most brutal elements in nature." But even as she is being trampled to death by the horse amid visions of planets, constellations, Ferris wheels; even as she lies there dying in the reflected glow of their burning house in Canada, she feels herself being lifted upward toward the stars, toward Orion, toward the Pleiades, Beatrice ascending to Paradise, soon to be joined there by her Dante. The life of a "good" woman has in the end once again saved a "lost" man.

Consul as Yvonne's "Armadillo." On her first ride with Hugh, Yvonne sees an armadillo that she wants to buy as a pet. Hugh tries to dissuade her by telling her that if she pets the thing loose in her garden, it'll tunnel into the ground and never come back. Moreover, he maintains, if she tries to stop it, "it will do its damnedest to pull you down the hole too" (p. 113). The point of the homily is apparently lost on her; she will still try to save the Consul from destroying himself. He is too content in his "garden"; he is also too well insulated against any of her attempts or entreaties. Yvonne is also too stubborn to recognize the signs, portents, and omens telling her that their marriage could never succeed. For instance, those signs in the Town House window that seemed to be changing in order to signal danger to her: "Informal Dancing in the Zebra Room" became "Infernal Dancing in the Zebra Room"; "Notice to Destroy Weeds" became "Notice to Newlyweds." Still she paid no heed; she would come to know the Consul's innocence and basic goodness, even if it had to be through consorting with the lecherous Laruelle (p. 264).

Door Left Open in the Mind. Somewhere Yvonne had read about the husband of an alcoholic woman who had been advised to join his wife in her drinking if he wished to help her toward a "cure". And so, on her first day back in Quauhnauhuac, when Geoffrey offers her a drink, she hesitates at first; she hates drinking, especially early in the morning. But "she undoubtedly should: it was what she had made up her mind to do if necessary, not to have one drink alone but a great many drinks with the Consul" (p. 47).

Later that day, at the Hotel Popo with Hugh, she agrees to having a drink, "Mescal, por favor," she says. "I've always wanted to find out what Geoffrey sees in it" (p. 326). The intention, albeit a belated one, is valid. In her extremity, wandering aimlessly in the dark forest amid the lightning and thunder, cold sober as she is, the mescal reveals to her the "door left open in the mind--as men have been known in great thunderstorms to leave their real doors open for Jesus to walk in...and it was through this mental door that Yvonne, still balancing herself on the log, now perceived that something was menacingly wrong" (p. 33). Too late, it seems, did that transcendental clairvoyance, that sobria inebriata that Geoffrey found in mescal, come to her. The rearing, threatening horse was already close by!

Games Hamlet Plays. The Oedipal puzzle becomes even more complicated when we learn that Yvonne's child by her first marriage was named Geoffrey. Upon the death of this child, Yvonne returned to Hollywood to try to resume the movie career she had begun as a thirteen-year-old leading lady to a cowboy star. (Cf. Hugh dressed in full American cowboy regalia at Tomalin.)

More Oedipalia: At the Salon Ofelia (we are now in Hamlet; Hamlet has rejected Ophelia because he is presumably in love with his mother, and so unconsciously resists his urge for his mother by rejecting Ophelia), Yvonne and Hugh go for a swim.

The Consul, who has been rejecting Yvonne in so many other ways, now begins ordering mescal to speed him on the road to self-destruction. The owner of the Salon tries to rescue the Consul by getting him to pray to the Virgin. While Geoffrey is praying for a return of his purity and for another chance with Yvonne (his Virgin?), his prayers are mockingly interrupted by the voices of Yvonne and Hugh planning their trip up Popocatepetl. Later, after several more mescals, the Consul accuses Hugh and Yvonne (in terms resonant of Othello this time) of planning to cuckold him.

Now we are back to *Hamlet* again. Geoffrey is Hamlet the father, Hugh is Hamlet the son, and Yvonne is Gertrude, wife to one, mother to the other. The "imagined" cuckoldry persists. In Chapter XII, Geoffrey returns to the Farolito where, on a previous binge, he had left some important "symbols": a packet of Yvonne's letters and a pipe, obviously a phallic symbol and here the temptation is to digress to Faulkner's Sanctuary, published in 1931, where the impotent Popeye tries to rape Temple Drake with his corncob pipe. By coincidence - or design - one of the would-be assassins accuses the Consul of being Al Capon, the omitted letter e no typographical error. If these two related symbols don't point up Geoffrey's impotence with Yvonne (produced by his fear of incest--Hamlet-Gertrude-Ophelia, or Consul-daughter), his successful act of inter-course with the young whore, Maria, should be more convincing. He had prayed to the Virgin Mary for a virgin Yvonne; he is willing to accept a non-virgin Maria in answer to his prayers. All of this leads one to believe that in the Consul, Lowry hasn't created a character any more mature and more sexually sophisticated than the Dana Hilliot in *Ultramine*. The Consul is essentially that same adolescent scared stiff of sex and syphilis, and sustaining his sexual purity (with the help of alcohol and masturbation) by worshipping the virgin Janet, the girl he left behind. One should also recall that in Chapter I of Under the Volcano, Laruelle tells us how the young Geoffrey Firmin, when discovered coming out of the Hell Bunker with one of the Taskerson girls, blushed so guiltily, although no sexual (or near-sexual) act had been consummated therein.

The Consul notices that Maria's body was "Yvonne's too, her legs, her breasts,…" (p. 349). Not much later, confronted with his would-be assassins, he thinks, "Ah, if Yvonne, if only as a daughter, who would understand and comfort him, could only be at his side now!" (p. 360). The Consul is a Hamlet indeed!

Woman Without A Cause. Having lived so long in a make-believe world created out of equal parts of tinsel-land Hollywood, her father's fantasy cum speculation instant riches, and the never-never quality of Hawaii, Yvonne eventually found herself to be a woman without faith, a woman without a cause. Her more recent preceptors - the Consul, Hugh, Laruelle - provided her with options of questionable validity. Laruelle was too much of the dissembler, the make-believer, the cynic. The Consul was too deep for her; he was too much of the mystic, too much of the uncontrolled dabbler in magic spells. Hugh seemed to offer the best route to a new faith - unselfish, selfless, humanitarian, international, cosmic, " - yes, even what she was now on the point of finding, and losing, a faith in a cause, was better than none" (p. 268). She would have to go along with Hugh, with no actual violation of her loyalty to Geoffrey, now her ex-husband.

Whose Shack, Whose Refuge? The thing to do, Hugh had suggested, "is to get out of Vancouver as far as possible." First, get out of Mexico, and, presumably, take Geoffrey with you. No rivalry there, no betrayal of one's trust to one's brother. Go down one of the inlets to some fishing village and buy a shack slap spang on the sea…" (pp. 121–122). Hugh was right; the change might do Geoffrey good; he might stop drinking; he might even resume writing that book and whatever it is that he has been non-writing all these years down in Mexico.

"Instantly Hugh's shack began to take form in her mind. But it was not a shack - it was a home!..." (p. 269). Trouble is, it's hard to tell whether it's Hugh's shack or Geoffrey's. To be sure, Hugh insisted that she go to Canada, to their "paradise," with Geoffrey; but by some queer mental twist, she kept referring to the dream shack as "Hugh's shack." Did she really want to escape from Mexico with Hugh, rather than with Geoffrey? There was the incident in the bullring, where Hugh proved absolutamente capable of coping with the bull (life), so differently from the way in which Geoffrey had botched up his life. Then there was Geoffrey's cause - vague, unreal, demon-motivated and demon-ridden. How could she relate to such a cause, a cause apparently already lost? On the other hand, Hugh's cause was idealistic, to be sure, but it was a losing, not a lost, cause.

Now she was being threatened by the horse, "rearing, poised over her, petrified in midair, a statue, somebody was sitting on the statue..." (p. 325). It was Huerta, or the drunkard, or the murderer,...it was the Consul... Then there was the vision of the house, the shack in the northern "paradise," on fire, and she and Geoffrey were inside the burning house. Why didn't the vision show her inside the burning house with Hugh? Should she have consented after all to go there with Hugh? Did Hugh symbolize life, and the Consul death? Too late to regret the wrong choice; the burning dream was fading away, even as she felt herself being borne towards the stars. Somehow she could never visualize Geoffrey as lover or husband; as father, yes.

Laruelle And The Appearance Of Reality. Jacques Laruelle, like the films he used to make, is "a purveyor of the appearance of reality." To use a very corny **cliche**, he believes only in real life. He doesn't believe in the need for the Consul's Promethean suffering, in the grandness of the Consul's battle against death, or in the invitation to a meaningful life proclaimed in the inscription outside his very own doorway: No se puede vivir sin amar. He is afraid of life, especially now that he has ceased to create his own false icons on the screen, and persists in attempting to shatter everyone else's icons, especially the Consul's.

Laruelle is both Chorus and Actor in the mini-epic (or mini-tragedy) of the Consul's "day of death." He is also Prologue. Through the reading of Faust's final soliloquy and the concluding chorus from Marlowe's Doctor Faustus, and the letter the Consul had written (but never sent) to Yvonne, he tells the audience what to expect in the ensuing eleven chapters - or reels. In his control over almost every aspect of the making of a film, he anticipates the auteur type of French filmmaker of the Fifties.

He is the failed artist, the maker of films long since forgotten. Now he dreams of making a modern version of Marlowe's Doctor Faustus, with Geoffrey Firmin pre-enacting the various scenes in real life before the director's very eyes. Let the critics then doubt the verisimilitude of his **epic**, cosmic drama! Laruelle is also the movie camera that records everything it sees, never forgets anything, and (with the aid of a projector or a wheel - any wheel, even a Ferris wheel) can play back everything it ever saw or knew. He is not omniscient or clairvoyant: he is more like the frozen (stop-action) past. He also conveniently indulges Lowry's long-standing interest in films.

Laruelle is the consummate materialist, sensualist, avoider of the harsher, more painful realities of life through illusion rather than through drink. He has no inkling of the Consul's supernatural quest, of his growing knowledge of mystical and magical powers. He looks and dresses in a self-indulgent manner - a dandy with a flabby waistline. In Chapter VII, he does finally admit that the Consul probably does see more clearly when drinking or suffering; but despite this "clairvoyance," the Consul still can't see or comprehend "the things so important to us despised sober people."

On a higher (or at least more metaphorical) level, Laruelle is characterized as a serpent and a seducer, a man both "false" and "engaging," a man apparently preoccupied with "the essence of some guilty secret" (Chapter VI). Jacques Laruelle, the avant-garde French movie director now preparing to go back to Paris before the War breaks out, and the Consul's boyhood chum, by coincidence (or artistic intention) happens to be living in this same remote Mexican province as does the Consul. His house resembles something that might have been dreamed up by a Hollywood set designer employed by pre-television M-G-M (Mas-Grande-Mejico). Laruelle's house (Chapter VII) symbolizes the Consul's devastated marriage. Laruelle, as "serpent," had lived and seduced Yvonne (Eve) there. The spiral staircases do not lead to heaven, the two angels are unreal and thus constitute part of the whole mockery of heaven.

By coincidence again (or artistic intention), Laruelle is planning to do a film on Faust (how much did Faust's "magic" help him avert his doom?). The film of course is never completed. Nevertheless, he reflects Lowry's interest in films (cf. Laruelle's interpretation of the backward-moving Ferris wheel both as Buddha wheel and movie reel) and in the Faust legend. In addition, his mere presence activates the Consul to some extent. However, whether it is the Consul, Laruelle, or Lowry himself, man is destined to fail in this life. Freedom from alcoholism or anxiety on the one hand, or an enviable endowment of youthful energy, good health, or creativity - failure is inevitable.

Vigil As Virgil. Is Doctor Vigil intended to remind us of Virgil, Dante's guide through the Inferno and Purgatorio (but not through Paradiso, since Virgil was not a Christian)? Very likely, since *The Divine Comedy* provides one of the two significant frames of reference in the novel (the other is the Garden of Eden myth). Yet Doctor Vigil, as a Christian, can guide the Consul to "Paradise." He offers to take him to Guanajuato (life), but the Consul chooses to go to Parian (death).

The character of Vigil is based on one of Lowry's close Mexican friends during his stay in Mexico in 1936–38. He is prescient enough to recognize that the Consul is in a state of anomie, despite his wife's return. He even predicts, unaware of what he is saying, as would a medium in a trance, the "longer journey even than this proposed one" that the Consul will take to Tomalin, and eventually to Parian. Within the actually few hours to the Farolito and the barranca, the Consul - or his soul - will take the "long day's journey" that every soul which has denied love must take. In a sense, Vigil is the voice of the future, as Laruelle is the voice of the past. Vigil is also the prophet of consciousness over mind. He tries to serve as the Consul's good angel (herein - is the analogy with Faust, torn between the counsels of his good and bad angels), the one who could save the Consul from the volcanic pyre toward which he is being ineluctably drawn.

De Profundis. Seated in the mingitorio, the toilet, after his brief, unprophylactic interlude with the whore Maria, he notices the advertisement for Doctor Vigil's service on the filthy walls - "Secret illnesses of both sexes... Sexual Disturbances... Sexual Debility Impotence..." The good angel indeed! How well Vigil understood him! But now it is already too late - half past sick by the cock or half past six by the clock - he is now about to tangle with his murderers a "cloacal Prometheus" impotent in more ways than the one in which an impersonal physician might have helped (p. 352).

Horseman Of The Apocalypse. The drunken horseman (Death, one of the Four Horseman of the Apocalypse?) seen by Laruelle (and others) may symbolize Firmin and/or mankind. The horseman, with the number 7 branded on the horse's rump, likewise adumbrates the murder of both the Indian and Yvonne. Geoffrey is described several times as being "strong as a horse" (ironically, very likely). He releases the horse which kills Yvonne in the end. Hugh and Yvonne ("cowboy star and leading lady") escape briefly from Geoffrey on horses. Yvonne (former leading lady to Hollywood cowboy stars) had once been threatened (in a film) in a canyon by 200 stampeding horses, but she has always had a premonition of a horse about to trample her to death. The horse (especially #7) is an apocalyptic figure of death.

On the fateful journey to Tomalin, the Consul and Hugh see from their bus a simple Indian dying on the roadside. "Companero," the Indian cries, pleading for help. (He is the same Indian seen earlier astride horse #7.) But the two Anglos know that, according to Mexican law, anyone found touching a dying man is charged with complicity; and so they don't try to help the dying man. (A silly, primitive, Mexican law? Compare it with the general reluctance of American physicians to treat any roadside casualty for fear of being charged with "malpractice" or "complicity" - unless there is a "Good Samaritan Law" in that state providing him with immunity.) The Indian dies, a pariah, an untouchable primitive segregated by a "civilized" law from "civilized" men. A few hours later, the Consul himself will re-enact the role of a pariah when he, too, will be dying; and a pariah dog will be thrown into the barranca with him; and the last word he will hear is companero.

We Are All Pelados. When the pelado is picked up at the first stop of the bus to Tomalin, he is considered to be just another drunken Mexican, eccentrically wearing two hats (layers of disguise?) and eating a melon (the fruits of Mexico?). The Consul then suggests that the pelado is really a Spanish Fascist working with the Mexican Union Militar. Later, when the pelado is seen clutching in his hand the bloodstained coins he has stolen from the dying Indian, the Consul and Hugh are convinced that the pelado represents not only the burgeoning power of a corrupt police force, but also the police force's sanction of any aggression against the wounded, the deprived, the indigent of Mexico. And Hugh, the Consul and Yvonne, are three Anglos, powerless to help the oppressed, reduced to impotence by the sentimental politics of their world.

Like the real vultures seen everywhere in Mexico, a human vulture, a pelado (literally a man peeled, or so stripped of all honor that he will prey even on the poor) steals the dead Indian's money. Wearing a homburg over a sombrero - the forced imposition of one culture over another? - the pelado reboards the bus and pays his fare with the stolen money. Again, as in the case of the dying Indian, the Consul's imminent murder is foreshadowed. He is later charged with being a pelado and a spy by the secret military police. A pelado, Si; a spy, No! Yes, he, too, has been a "pilferer of meaningless muddled ideas out of which his rejection of his life had grown, who had worn his two or three bowler hats, his disguises over his abstractions..."

Flawed Cervantes To Flawed Quixote. The Consul's drinking is not characteristic of ordinary drunkenness. True, he feels guilty about being constantly borracho, but it is this same drunkenness, these frequent stupors, that frees his language so that it approaches poetry. In the same way, madness evoked poetry in Lear, and chivalry did the same for Cervantes (in *Don Quixote*). "A shabby little man with a black shade over one eye, wearing a black coat, but a beautiful sombrero with long gay tassels down the back..." - this was Cervantes, proprietor of the Salon Ofelia. "Was this the face that launched five hundred ships, and betrayed Christ into being in the Western Hemisphere?" The paraphrase of the Marlowe line is impressive, but this Cervantes claims that he is Tlaxcalan, not Spanish, and can't say for sure whether he is distantly descended from the original Cervantes or from any of the original Spanish conquistadores who brought Christianity to Mexico. But he could be, since the Tlaxcalans did collaborate with the Spanish invaders. In any event, he is first of all interested in serving the Consul with all the drink he wishes. Then, he would like to interest the Consul in his fighting cock, but the Consul is made uncomfortable by the sight of the bird. Cock fights remind him of "the vicious little man-made battles, cruel and destructive, yet somehow bedraggedly inconclusive, each brief as some hideously mismanaged act of intercourse,..." (p. 287). The fighting cock is also a Cabbalistic symbol of death and atonement. (Is this what Cervantes is unconsciously offering the Consul?) For Geoffrey, however, it takes on its more vulgar **connotation** (penis), and thus becomes a symbol of his own impotence with Yvonne earlier in the day. Later ("half past six by the clock"), it becomes a symbol of his impotence in the face of death: "Sick...half past sick by the cock," an unintended feeble (but prophetic) pun (p. 352).

Now Cervantes wants to show his Don Quixote his private apartment, especially a little shrine to the Virgin at which the Consul can pray. And the Consul does, as if to prove that Cervantes (through the symbol of the cock) had actually offered him atonement first, and then death. The Consul, Yvonne, and Hugh dine rather well at the table set by the host. For the Consul, every dish has some pornographic meaning. As for Cervantes, all the Consul wants of him now are mescal, more information about Tlaxcala, perhaps a cleansing stone in the toilet, and assistance in trying to convince Yvonne and Hugh to join him on a trip to Tlaxcala after they leave Tomalin. When Hugh refuses, Tlaxcala is out and Parian and death are inevitable. The Consul's fate is sealed when Cervantes reminds the trio that "the fantasy is that when three friends take fire with the same match, the last dies before the other two" (p. 306). To the very end, this Cervantes tried to save his Don Quixote. But the real Don Quixote was Hugh, the idealist, the fighter for all causes, lost or otherwise, the singer of revolutionary songs - "Hijos del pueblo que oprimen cadenas" - Children of the people who impose chains - "esa injusticia no debe existir" - that injustice should not be permitted to be...(p. 334). But the Consul continued to argue for non-interference in the affairs of other nations. And the Consul achieves death (after atonement) first! Is he therefore the real Don Quixote? Is there after all a bit of the Christ in Don Quixote, and a bit of the Don Quixote in Christ? Or, in the most simplistic terms, is there any real difference between Geoffrey and Hugh? Are they not, after all, one?

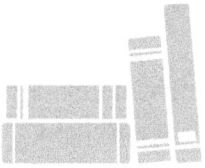

UNDER THE VOLCANO

CRITICISM

There is little disagreement among the critics that Malcolm Lowry was a literary narcissist, a monomaniac, an egotist, a solipsist, a man who throughout all his writing begged to be loved and admired by others as much as he loved and admired himself. After *Under the Volcano*, the reader is ready to cry out, Enough! at the replications of the Lowry ego in the subsequent long pieces of fiction. There never was enough of a distance between Lowry and his "autobiographical sharings." John Wain, for example, has said that what is so objectionable about much of today's fiction is that "for the first time the artist is content to gather his evidence from the self and leave it at that." Even Hemingway, that consummate egotist, could frequently conceive of a hero other than Hemingway himself.

In Dark As the Grave Wherein My Friend Is Laid, Lowry reaches the peak of literary narcissism in once again assuming the obvious role of a "writer writing about writers writing about books in which they are the main characters." Perhaps one critic was not too far off the mark in characterizing such writing as masturbatory rather than narcissistic. On the other hand, William Gass is happy with the fact that Lowry was never subtle (or fairly never); that he made no effort to "maintain a figurative distance between author, work, and reader,...resisting every effort at literal interpretation" (Fiction and the Figures of Life). Stendhal spoke of the function of the novelist as that of a mirror in the roadway; but it was true of Stendhal, as it was of Lowry, that the mirror reflected "only his own reactions to what was passing"; as such, the picture of these reactions had, it must be admitted, total fidelity.

Lowry's unfinished work should have been left unfinished. What he did leave unfinished (or unassembled) shows that he had already moved far beyond the novel form, and that no well-intentioned widow, publisher, or friend should have tried to create novels out of the mass of subjective, autobiographic notes, commentaries, travelogues, quasi-confessionals, and literary experiments that he left behind. The Schubert "Unfinished Symphony" has remained to this day unedited, intact, an "unfinished" symphony only in the conventional sense. Must a symphony have four movements? Schubert's "Unfinished" has but two, Sibelius' Fourth Symphony is all in one movement. When some enterprising musicologists tried to piece together a Tchaikovsky "Seventh" Symphony out of fragments and "bones" that were found among his musical effects, they came up with what could be called at best a near-symphony, a thing of shreds and patches. Let us, therefore, accept Lowry as a one-novel writer, and consider ourselves fortunate that that one novel was a masterpiece.

GENERAL CRITICISM

Aiken On Lowry. Lowry's official biographer, Douglas Day, concludes that Lowry "was not really a novelist, except by accident." The sum total of Lowry's varied talents other than writing further convinces Day that Lowry was an autobiographer. One may add that by classifying *Under the Volcano* (and much of Lowry's other works) as fiction, Lowry (and his sympathetic widow, friends, editors) was copping out; that he refused to take the rap for what the Consul, Sigbjorne Wilderness, Ethan Llewelyn, and other personae did. One such editor has said that one could distinguish Lowry from the Consul, for example, in that "the Consul is a fictional artifact, triumphant in his fall, and Lowry, the man, died an alcoholic's death, his torments unresolved." Conrad Aiken has said that he (Aiken) was the side of the Consul that still hoped for deliverance in a continuing search for Eridanus, but that it was Lowry himself who contributed the self-destructive element in the Consul that sought out the barranca despite all the ministrations of those around him. Lowry, Aiken added, "really wished for the unconscious - the womb, if you will, and nothing any of us could do for him changed that" (Richard Costa, Malcolm Lowry).

Bradbrook On Lowry As Expatriate. Lowry may be compared with that other celebrated expatriate, Samuel Beckett. Both writers manifest the strength, tolerance, and compassion needed to survive in an alien world. "A self-destructive world," says Bradbrook, "can be lived in only by those who do not take refuge in stoic rigidity..." They have the courage to accept the breaking up of their identities, and it is this courage which provides them with the basis on which to construct their art. "The broken life is not necessarily the weak life..." (M. C. Bradbrook, *Literature in Action*).

Johnson And The Tyranny Of Style. "If Mr. Lowry would sieve out his style a bit, and prune the abandoned brilliant image," Elizabeth Johnson wrote (Commonweal, 3/7/47), "I think he would not be just an 'interesting' author of promise, but an outstanding writer." The desire or the ability to prune were far beyond the Lowry style which early in his career assumed the wildly and brilliantly colorful lushness of the Mexican landscape and never relinquished it, even in the more austere, sober reaches of Canada.

Allen On Symbolism As Pastiche. Like Johnson and other critics, Walter Allen finds himself too uncomfortable with the prodigality of Lowry's style. It is for him "out of Djuna Barnes by Henry James." It is a style that employs every technical device incorporated into the experimental novel since Laurence Sterne and James Joyce, and it employs them with the greatest of skill. It is a style that employs every possibility of symbolism that situation and setting will allow. After a while, the symbolism becomes a little too pat, too predictable. In the end, "while it makes for an agonizing concentration of the tragedy, together with the other factors of characterization, style and method, it makes also for an inescapable impression of pastiche" (New Statesman and Nation, 12/6/47).

Widmer On Lowry. Although Lowry came to Canada late in his short lifetime and was a Canadian by adoption only, many of the critical efforts (especially by Canadian critics) to make him a "Canadian" writer are less than convincing, suggests Eleanor Widmer. For one thing, Lowry's background was a cosmopolitan one, embracing England, Norway, Paris, the U. S., and, of course, Mexico. In fact, his life and his writings were so inextricably involved with the U. S. and Mexico that it might be most advisable to categorize his major works as "hemispheric." Lowry, Katherine Anne Porter, and Willa Cather may represent the first of a new class of writers, not distinctly or exclusively concerned with their own countries, "but with the inter-relationships of American cultures" ("The Drunken Wheel: Malcolm Lowry and *Under the Volcano*," in The Forties: Fiction, Poetry, Drama, ed. Warren French).

REVIEWS

Mark Schorer. This reviewer was obviously most impressed with Lowry's exuberant style, with the unmistakable delight the writer took in what he wrote and in what other writers had written. There is vigor and dash in Lowry's writing, and "he creates, through his style no less than through his acute capacity for sensuous observation, a novel of opulent texture and consequently resonant meaning." Schorer doesn't hesitate to compare Lowry with James Joyce, especially for the primary experience that the young writer was able to bring into his fiction (New York Herald Tribune Weekly Book Review, 2/23/74).

Eleanor Clark. The patent weaknesses in the novel are far outweighed by the vigor and impact that Lowry has brought to the novel. He is to be commended for having written a large and ambitious novel, occasionally very sad;...despite a "specific failure of vision and at times...a more irritating subjectivity, the book would compel respect if only for its more than occasional skill and for the conglomerate wealth of perceptions that has gone into it" (The Nation, 3/22/47).

"Times" Of London Literary Supplement. The book is neither a morbid nor a minor achievement. Whatever morbidity there may be in it is "akin to that of Elizabethan tragedy, born of an involved and passionate interest in the secrets of the fall of man." The light the author casts upon the Consul casts a shadow of tragic dimensions (8/20/47).

D. S. Savage. The novel has many defects. Nevertheless, it is without doubt "the most interesting, the most perceptive, and the most promising novel it has fallen to my lot to review so far this year" (The Spectator, 10/10/47).

"The New Yorker." The writer is passionately serious about what he has to say about the hopes and fears of humankind. But earnestness aside, Lowry has succeeded "only in writing a rather good imitation of an important novel" (2/22/47).

H. R. Hays. There are many obscurities in this novel, but they do not outscore the rich variety of meaning the reader can find on many levels. The style is both poetic and virile, the insights are frequently profound. It has the capacity to move anyone who seeks for an honest and passionate approach to human experience" (*The New York Times*, 2/23/74).

John Woodburn. "I have never before used the word in a review,... but I am of the opinion... that *Under the Volcano* is a work of genius" (*Saturday Review of Literature*, 2/22/47).

CRITICISM

Spender On Lowry And Dante. The novel takes on the dimensions of an authentic modern tragedy with the murder of the Consul. Up to that point, his life had lacked a convincing affirmation of the values which he knew, with which he had grown up, and which in his very own consciousness he never actually did destroy. The Consul always showed genuine concern for the values "which are outside the time in a world entirely contemporary," says Stephen Spender, and which are "resolved in the **theme** of *the Divine Comedy*, the progress of the soul" (Introduction to *Under the Volcano*).

Kazin On The "Timelessness" Of "*Under The Volcano.*" If a masterpiece is to be judged properly, says Alfred Kazin, it must be tested both for originality of powers and for a "kind of inviolability from the age." In this respect, Lowry's masterpiece may be favorably compared with Nabokov's *Pale Fire* as a "unique invention in the early 20th-Century 'modern' manner - the last thoroughly successful instance was Malcolm Lowry's *Under the Volcano* (1947)." (As quoted by Eleanor Widmer in "The Drunken Wheel: Malcolm Lowry and *Under the Volcano*.")

W. H. New On Lowry As A Christian Moralist. Lowry has often been classified as an esoteric symbolist along with such other writers as Rimbaud, Yeats, and D. H. Lawrence. However, where those three avoided at any cost incorporating any religious judgments or moral overtones, Lowry for his part chose to reinforce his kind of symbolism with the strict Methodist concepts of sin, purgatory, and redemption with which he had been brought up. The religious guidelines are there, taken literally from Bunyan and Dante, more metaphorically from Kafka, Marlowe, and Dostoevsky. "Essentially (if one adds to these the overwhelming influence of the Cabbala)," "says W. H. New, "Under the Volcano represents a medieval view of man's moral predicament" (*Articulating West: Essays on Purpose and Form in Modern Canadian Literature*).

Widmer On Lowry's "Doomsday Book." When measured against the facts of his own life, Lowry's *Under the Volcano* becomes a self-fulfilling prophecy. Within and outside the novel, there is the inevitable statement of man's sense of dispossession, of alienation from himself and the world around him. The novel, like Lowry's life, is an alcoholic nightmare, a cultivated but nonetheless bitter reflection on a life eternally threatened with, and surrounded by, meaninglessness. Nevertheless, it remains a dazzling display of "everything Lowry knew or had read, believed, doubted, praised, or could evoke," says Eleanor Widmer. It evolves in the end a sort of "doomsday book, a catechism, a performer of magic, and a prayer."

But it is just that "dazzling display," that eclectic grab bag of too many disparate elements that in time becomes obsessive. Lowry will let no motif or **metaphor** go; instead, he attempts to "weld into cohesiveness ornate occultism with an analytic statement on modern man, the belief in the eternal wheel with the transitory Mexican journey of one lonely soul" ("The Drunken Wheel").

Novel As Hallucination. If we can forget for a moment Lowry's powerful compulsion to make everything he wrote autobiographic, then *Under the Volcano* may be construed as an attempt to achieve a religious or spiritual revelation through experimentation with hallucinogenic materials. On this premise, every incident in the novel is a hallucination. Lowry may have anticipated Aldous Huxley (or followed Coleridge and De Quincey) who actually did experiment with mescalin (cf. mescal-mescalin) either to heighten his literary sensitivities or to discover new truths. The drunkenness of the Consul cannot be considered merely as alcoholic self-indulgence (Richard Costa, Malcolm Lowry).

Lowry As Jungian Artist. At the end of a most unproductive session, a well-known Freudian psychiatrist said to his patient, "When you come back tomorrow, bring me a dream." This same psychiatrist claimed that he went to the movies about three times a week because, he said, "You will find some of the most typical American dreams in the films people watch." Lowry is said to have believed that a dream was to the dreamer as a film was to the viewer. In this respect he was echoing not only the Freudian movie fan above but that Freudian "defector," Carl Jung, as well. Jung believed that dreams were more absorbing than conscious life. Dreams were also throwbacks to the "collective unconscious," "primordial images," "archetypal fragments." Dreams, in short, are not always exclusively subjective and based solely on the dreamer's personal experiences. Lowry, like many another artist, could draw from "the matrix of a mythopoeic imagination that has vanished from our rational age" that Jung found in the unconscious (Costa).

Film As Dream Factory. Lowry often uses dreams and film interchangeably. His characters are often preoccupied with waking and half-waking (with or without mescal) visions (less often, dreams) fixed in time and space as "on the screen of his mind," or as if a motion picture had been projected onto a static, still picture, painting, or drawing. The technique is somewhat similar to the "animated" figures superimposed on a previously prepared background in the making of animated film cartoons. The effect achieved this way (as Lowry saw it) was a "fixed, timeless, haunted background, but this was not part of what was going on, this was only the relief against which it could be seen, the means by which it became visible." Against a fixed background of archetypal motifs, Laruelle (Lowry) projects the events of the year before. The wheel is to be seen as a reel of film. In the eleven remaining chapters, the reader "sees" what went on; the "fixed, timeless, haunted background" helps him "understand" what he is seeing. The images, visions, "mind explosions" produced by this superimposition are the substance of whatever explication of the novel is possible (Costa).

Art As Neurosis. "When a form of 'art' is primarily personal," said Jung, "it deserves to be treated as if it were a neurosis." Jung at one time offered to analyze Lowry merely on the basis of having read *Under the Volcano*. Lowry never agreed to it, probably feeling, as did Hemingway, that (to paraphrase Hemingway) "analysis might effect a cure, but the patient - the artist - would die." Today, with psychoanalysis a working tool for many artists, such a reservation sounds almost ludicrous. "What is essential in a work of art," Jung wisely asserted, "is that it should rise far above the realm of personal life and speak from the spirit and heart of mankind." In this respect, *Under the Volcano* succeeds more often than it fails (Costa).

Dodson On "Volcano" As Ironies. Daniel B. Dodson briefly summarizes the novel as "a cluster of intricately related ironies: a homecoming and a final leavetaking; restoration and deprivation; love offered and love betrayed; life affirmed while it is being brutally denied; a quest which has already ended." Like Jacques Barzun, Dodson also found that after a second reading of the novel, it became more than an "anthology of literary styles," references, reminiscences, and "resonances" of books past. It is not fictional account of drunkenness (an assertion that cannot be repeated too often), either the Consul's or Lowry's. Drunkenness is, to be sure, the **theme**, but it is not the drunkenness of a Don Birham (in Charles Jackson's *The Lost Weekend*). It is the drunkenness of Geofrey Firmin, correlated with the drunkenness of the world as seen by a Dostoevsky or a Hermann Hesse; a world "reeling down the corridors of disaster filled with the sins of both commission and, particularly, omission"; the drunkenness of a world which has opted for impotence and disengagement in "the dark night presided over by palpable evil." (Malcolm Lowry).

William Gass. "Although *Under the Volcano* has many flaws, it is strong where most recent novels are weak: it has no fear of feeling." In Lowry's Mexico "for the mind," there are no menacing volcanoes, Gass observes, "only menacing phrases, where complex chains of concepts traverse our consciousness..." In effect, he is not describing an actual Mexico, but creating one. In Lowry's Mexico, events and incidents take place at the very moment that we are reading about them in a manner wholly contrary to the historical process - "over and over as it may be, irregularly even, at widely separated times - whenever we restore these notes to music" (Fiction and the Figures of Life).

UNDER THE VOLCANO

ESSAY QUESTIONS AND ANSWERS

Question: Some critics have seen in *Under the Volcano* more than a study of one man's debauchery, dissoluteness, and disintegration. They view it as an extremely moral tale, an extended elaboration of the Christian belief that "The meek shall inherit the earth." Are we dealing, then, with a Christian novel as parable?

Answer: There is little disagreement among Lowry scholars that *Under the Volcano* is (and was intended to be) a Christian novel; that is, a novel treating (albeit broadly) the **theme** of Original Sin in the Garden of Eden, and the New Testament parable of the Good Samaritan. But we find still another explicit affirmation of Christian faith (however tardy), when the Consul, desperately trying to retrieve Yvonne's letters from his would-be assassins, says (perhaps without knowing exactly what he is saying): "Only the poor, only through God, only the people you wipe your feet on, the poor in spirit, old men carrying their fathers and philosophers weeping in the dust, America perhaps, Don Quixote." This statement immediately places the Consul on the side of the meek and the humble, and also on the side of the loyal and the devoted, the compassionate, the democratic, the idealistic. In such a statement, one finds the moral and spiritual thrust of the Beatitudes almost completely restated.

Consider, for one, the poor, poor in worldly goods, poor in spirit. For them, God has prepared and reserved a fitting reward; in truth, the meek shall in due time come into their inheritance, the earth. Neither will these same poor (or others equally devoted to the past and to older generations) go unrewarded for literally (and figuratively) carrying their father on their backs. The past is an unavoidable burden; unfortunately, those who are best equipped to carry the burden of the past refuse to do so; the poor, however, rarely have the option of refusing this, or other, burdens. The image is vividly recorded by Lowry: "...an old lame Indian was carrying on his back...another poor Indian, yet older and more decrepit than himself. He carried the older man and his crutches, trembling in every limb under the weight of the past, he carried both the burdens" (Italics added). Mexico, like so many other ancient lands, must also bear up under the weight of the past, a truth which, both in its historical and spiritual sense, the Consul came to realize rather late.

Who else will redeem us, besides the poor? The philosophers; not, however, the philosopher kings, but the demotic, compassionate ones, those who weep in the dust. There is essentially nothing aristocratic or exclusive about the Consul's (Lowry's) redeemers of mankind; humility is the watchword, compassion is the battle cry, love is the motto emblazoned on every heart. Between the unworldly philosophers and the equally unworldly Don Quixotes, the Consul finds democratic America, pragmatically idealistic, idealistically pragmatic, as still another potential redeemer of mankind. The notion of a 1938 America (with her nonintervention policy toward civil-war-torn Spain) as a compassionate, disinterested force for universal melioration and redemption is both ambiguous and fascinating.

Be that as it may, America, too, can be part of the grand design of human redemption through the poor, the humble, the meek, the quixotic, the compassionate. Every Indian dying by the wayside is a Christ crucified. Every old man carrying another old man on his back is a Christ carrying a cross on the road to Calvary. In respect to the whole concept of redemption and salvation, the Consul is as Christian and as theologically orthodox as the most enthusiastic of Calvinist hymn-singers. *Under the Volcano* is definitely a Christian novel as parable.

Question: The Consul is obviously no ordinary, uncomplicated dipsomaniac. He drinks heavily, and knows that he does; he neither enjoys nor approves of his heavy drinking. Then why does he continue to drink, and to avoid all possible help to stop himself from drinking?

Answer: "Whosoever unceasingly strives upward...him can we save" is the quotation from Goethe that serves as one of the three epigraphs of the novel. Only when one strives upward, the Consul believes, do all the "features" of life then seem "to grow more clear, more animated, friends and enemies more identifiable, special problems, scenes, and with them the sense of his own reality, more separate from [oneself]." "Los Borrachones," that picture of master drunkards hanging on Laruelle's wall, might be said to convey that same message, and in a highly lurid way. Could these drunkards, somehow separated from their demanding bodies, be seen as spirits becoming freer, more distinctive, more noble, the higher they ascended into the light? If they could strive upward, why couldn't he?

The Consul had thought about going into a sanatorium where he could "dry out," be cured of his obsessive drinking. He had to leave Quauhnauhuac; there was something about the place that paralyzed his will - the will to stop drinking, the will to strive upward. "No angels nor Yvonne nor Hugh could help him here." The demons were inside him as well as outside; he was bound to them. Laruelle couldn't help noticing how these same demons kept him from attempting a reconciliation with Yvonne: "...And that you treat her indifferently as this, and still continue only to care where the next drink's coming from?"

Yvonne could help him. He recalled that when he had striven upwards, during the early days of his relationship with Yvonne, everything seemed clearer, and he was more capable of identifying himself and his world. The mere act of soliciting and accepting Yvonne's help - her very presence, her very companionship gave - him the desire and the will to look toward the light. But Yvonne was also offering him love, and this he could not accept from her. Hence the indifference toward her, and the continuing concern with where the next drink's coming from. Yes, the drinking was an antidote to her love, to the will to strive upwards, to be saved. Alcohol not only narcotized; it also immunized.

The Consul drank because he had learned his Calvinist Sunday-School-lessons well. He was predestined to end up in Hell. If so, there was no point in striving upwards, in accepting Yvonne's love and help. He was predestined; a quick "replay" of the day's events proved it: Yvonne's arrival; the snake in the garden; the quarrels with Laruelle, Hugh, and Yvonne; the infernal machine; the meeting with Senora Gregorio; the finding of Yvonne's letters; "and much beside, how all the events of the day indeed had been as indifferent tufts of grass he had half-heartedly clutched at or stones loosed on his downward flight, which were still showering on him from above." He could see the Chief of Gardens and the Chief of Rostrums waiting by the telephone. The telephone would soon confirm his fate, the fate that no angels, no loving persons, no free will, could interdict.

Earlier that day, he had studied the painting called "Los Borrachones" (actually it was an old prohibitionist poster): "Down, headlong into hades, selfish and florid-faced, into a tumult of fire-spangled fiends;...shrieking among falling bottles and emblems of broken hopes, plunged the drunkards;..." There was something ludicrous about the poster, about the angels shielding males, males shielding females, the "saved" mixed (or confused) with the "lost." The Consult took another look at the poster, and "Suddenly he felt something never felt before with such shocking certainty. It was that he was in hell himself." And he knew that for him it would have to be Parian and the Farolito, "the lighthouse that invited the storm."

Question: Although Laruelle as a former film director seems to be the logical representative of Lowry's familiarity with, and reliance upon, film techniques, there is much to be said for Yvonne as a more visible manifestation of Lowry's interest in films. Show how Yvonne, in her former role as movie star, and in her latter role as "love goddess," personifies the film ethos in *Under the Volcano*.

Answer: When one speaks of Yvonne, one must per force speak of three not one, personifications. She is Yvonne Constable, Hawaii-born daughter of Captain Constable, adventurer and speculator, and late consul to Iquique; Yvonne Griffaton, dramatic movie star; Yvonne Firmin, married to a dissolute, alcohol-ridden consul in Quauhnauhuac, Mexico. Then again, as Yvonne Firmin, she is still two more personifications: she is a "love goddess," unpossessible to Geoffrey, Hugh, and Laruelle; she is also Beatrice, trying to save a Dante from his predestined hell for the much-desired paradise. If she can play the part of a "good woman," then her love may yet save Geoffrey from the infernal fate for which he has been predestined. In short, there are three "faces" to Yvonne.

But because Yvonne is such a fantasy figure, one must look to the apotheosis of fantasy land, Hollywood, to trace the development of Yvonne from simple Hawaiian-born, all-round outdoor girl, to the "love goddess" pursued by Geoffrey, Hugh, and Laruelle in Quauhnauhuac. The Yvonne married to the Consul, Yvonne Firmin, can never separate herself completely from the Yvonne Constable, the unmarried daughter of the highly unsuccessful Captain Constable, or from Yvonne Griffaton, the fairly successful Hollywood actress. Yvonne was once a child movie star, an extremely competent horsewoman (she had performed her own stunts in films), a natural beauty.

After her first marriage (to Cliff Wright) and the death of her child, Yvonne went back to Hollywood. Not without some trepidation, of course; would enough fans (and Hollywood executives) remember her: at fifteen, the leading lady for Bill Hodson, the cowboy star, in three films? Would enough people remember her as the genuine outdoor girl out of Hawaii, the expert swimmer, golfer, dancer, and equestrienne? Youth is a very valuable commodity in Hollywood, and Yvonne at twenty-four, a honey-tanned Venus, is a twenty-four-year-old "Boomp Girl," aged by the calendar and personal tragedy, so that she may not be as acceptable to the public now as she was as a twelve-year-old, war-whooping tomboy, or a fourteen-year-old child-actress but one year away from becoming the leading lady to cowboy hero Bill Hodson. Now she is back in Hollywood, a sober twenty-four-year-old, with no time now for love in her life; her work is everything, and the studio likes the new Yvonne Constable, the "Boomp Girl" turned dramatic actress. But the studio does not truly accept the new Yvonne Constable (or Yvonne Griffaton); only in the mind of her publicity agent is she well on the way to becoming Hollywood's greatest dramatic actress, well on the way to becoming a star for the second time. Promises are not equivalent to roles. "For her ambitions as an actress had always been somewhat spurious: they suffered in some sense from the dislocations of the functions - she saw this - of womanhood itself." In nine short years, she had outgrown Hollywood.

Now she was Yvonne Firmin, ex-actress, talking to Jacques Laruelle, ex-film director, reminiscing about the year 1932, when they had both been at the same party, "outdoor-barbecue-swimming pool-and-bar in Hollywood." In due time, both ex-habitues of "Tinsel Land" exchanged photographic mementos of their cinematic triumphs (a confidence not to be shared with the more "spiritual" Consul). For with Laruelle she could once again become Yvonne Griffaton, the most real "unreal" of all the Yvonnes in her art-as-life repertoire. Once upon a time, Le Destin de Yvonne Griffaton was the ultimate gloss on the life of Yvonne Constable; with Geoffrey Firmin, however, there was no place for Yvonne Griffaton - she was much too real for the fantasy world he seemed to be inhabiting. She - whether as Yvonne Constable or Yvonne Griffaton - had the will, but not the faith; the Consul, on the other hand, had the faith, but not the will.

And so, in the middle years (or was it the later years, since we are here concerned with the professional lifetime of a former child movie star?) of her career, Yvonne was about to assume two highly dramatic roles - that of "love goddess" (a "natural" for a movie actress, although as a leading lady to a cowboy star there were very few occasions for emoting passionately), and that of an awkward Beatrice to an equally clumsy Dante. As a stricken love goddess, desired by Geoffrey (when sober), Hugh, and Laruelle, she is (spiritually) unpossessible to all three because of the imperfectability of love. No se puede vivir sin amar - Life is impossible without love - one of the main **themes** of the novel asserts. But for Yvonne - and for many others - true love is, after all, to be found only on the silver screen, in the magic land of the cinema.

Although Yvonne apparently enjoyed the love-goddess role (with only occasional, slight qualms of guilt over her infidelity toward her husband), there is much evidence to indicate that she couldn't throw herself into the role of redemptive "good woman" with the same kind of unself-conscious expertise that she could draw upon for the role of love goddess. After all, "love goddess," "love object," "screen siren," "sexpot" had been (and still are) part of the stock-in-trade of the cinema everywhere; but how does one play the part of the redemptive "good woman" convincingly (Beatrice or Marguerite - to a film director, the roles are interchangeable) to a man who doesn't know whether he is Dante or Faust - or Christ? (The scenario, moreover, as she read it, or as the "director" explained it to her, made no mention of a Mary Magdalena!) Life, it seemed, had drawn too far away from the more palpable "reality" of the cinema, and Yvonne too many years before the era of Ingmar Bergman) just couldn't adapt her limited acting resources to the non-representational, symbolic drama that the Consul, her present "leading man," was preparing to perform in. Yvonne, used to dressing in fringed leather shirts, riding breeches, high-heeled boots, and wearing a ten-gallon Stetson, felt much too uncomfortable, too much out of character, in the ennobling, gauzy, transparent robes of a Beatrice, a Marguerite - or a Mary Magdalene. Given the option, she would much prefer acting opposite Hugh, "his cowboy hat on the back of his head, his feet in their high-heeled boots on the seat in front," in the Arena Tomalin. The indisputable tragedy is that child stars must eventually grow up!

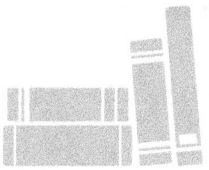

BIBLIOGRAPHY

The most complete bibliography to date of Malcolm Lowry biography, criticism, and review is Earle Birney's compilation of such materials in four issues of *Canadian Literature*, a quarterly of criticism and review, published by the University of British Columbia (George Woodcock, editor). The compilation comprises Issue 8 (Spring, 1961, 80–88); Issue 9 (Summer, 1961, 80–84); Issue 11 (Winter, 1962, 90–95; Issue 19 Winter, 1964, 83–89). A slightly more extensive bibliography (actually a "spin-off" of the Birney compilation) is J. Howard Woolmer's *A Malcolm Lowry Catalogue*. This 65-page booklet, No. 2 of Mr. Woolmer's *Focus Series* (New York: Woolmer, 1969), and the Birney compilation may be supplemented to a considerable extent by the complete and important collection of Lowry papers, fragments, memorabilia in the Special Collections Division of the University of British Columbia Library in Vancouver, British Columbia, Canada. Among these papers are the manuscripts of three incomplete Lowry novels: *La Mordida, The Ordeal of Sigbjorn Wilderness,* and *Dark As the Grave Wherein My Friend Is Laid.* The last manuscript has since been published in 1968, edited by Margerie Bonner Lowry and Douglas Day, official biographer of Malcolm Lowry.

A complete list of all of Lowry's published works will be found in the section of this Note under Chronology.

BIOGRAPHY AND MEMOIRS

The authorized biography is Douglas Day's *Malcolm Lowry*, New York: Oxford University Press, 1973. *The Selected Letters*, edited by Harvey Breit and Margerie B. Lowry, is published by J. B. Lippincott, New York and Philadelphia, 1965.

Aiken, Conrad. Editorial letter. *London Times Literary Supplement* (2/16/67), 127. Indispensable to an understanding of the inestimable influence Aiken had on Lowry's development as a writer. Aiken is generous, but not altogether forgiving of Lowry's "parasitism."

Bradbrook, Muriel. *Malcolm Lowry: His Art and Early Work*. New York: Cambridge University Press, 1974. An extremely valuable addition to the Lowry bibliography on three counts: (1) the writer is a fellow Liverpudlian, and was also a contemporary of Lowry's at Cambridge; (2) the writer recognizes the enormous importance of Lowry's own experiences in any attempt to understand his books; (3) the post-Volcano Lowry is not ignored, nor is he overpraised.

Breit, Harvey. "In and Out of Books - Obituary." *New York Times Book Review*, (7/14/57). Eulogistic, as one would expect of someone who was later to assist in the editing of Lowry's letters (1962).

Kirk, Downie. "More Than Music - Glimpses of Malcolm Lowry," *Canadian Literature* No. 8 (Spring, 1961), 31–38. One of several pieces in recent years contributing to the building up of Lowry as a Canadian writer.

Knickerbocker, Conrad. "Swinging the Paradise Street Blues: Malcolm Lowry in England." *Best Magazine Articles*: 1967. Gerald Walker, ed. (New York: Crown, 1967), 64–65. A good but insufficient contribution to the story of Lowry's down-and-out days in England.

_____. "The Voyages of Malcolm Lowry," *Prairie Schooner* (Winter, 1963), 301–14. A short but comprehensive "life" of Lowry which Knickerbocker was about to expand into an official biography. Much of this material was later incorporated into the official biography written by Douglas Day (1973).

Lorenz, Clarissa. "Call It Misadventure." *The Atlantic* (June, 1970), 106–12. For this writer, Lowry was an extremely gifted shlemazl.

Markson, David. "Malcolm Lowry: A Reminiscence." *The Nation* (2/7/66), 164–67. Markson carried on a lengthy correspondence with Lowry, and for this reason, what he has to say about Lowry is firsthand and authentic.

New, W. H. "Lowry's Reading: An Introductory Essay," *Canadian Literature* No. 44 (Spring, 1970), 5–12. An attempt to trace Lowry's literary influences in the way in which J. L. Lowes did the influences on Coleridge's *The Ancient Mariner and Kubla Khan*. Special emphasis is laid on the Cabbala and other works on mysticism.

Noxon, Gerald. "Malcolm Lowry: 1930." *Prairie Schooner* (Winter, 1963), 315–20. One of Lowry's oldest friends. When his Dollarton shack burned down, Lowry and his wife came to live with Noxon at Niagara-on-the-Lake, Ontario. (See account of this interlude in *October Ferry to Gabriola*.)

Stern, James. "Malcolm Lowry: A First Impression." *Encounter*, XXIX (September, 1967), 58–68. Interesting because Stern reports much of the advice Lowry gave to him when he [Stern] was starting out as a novelist.

CRITICAL STUDIES

There are only two book-length studies of Lowry's works thus far: Perle S. Epstein's *The Private Labyrinth of Malcolm Lowry: "Under the Volcano" and the Cabbala* (New York: Holt, Rinehart & Winston, 1969), and Richard H. Costa's *Malcolm Lowry* (New York: Twayne Publishers, Inc., 1972). The first is an incomplete investigation into the influences of the Cabbala and Mexican folklore (with some incidental digressions into the field of general mythology) on Lowry's novel. Some critics have reservations about Mrs. Epstein's evaluation of the Cabbala as an influence but this should not detract from the overall thoroughness of the research itself. The Costa book is equally thorough in its research, scholarship, and objectivity. But here too there are critics who feel that Costa has been too "compassionate" toward Lowry's "borrowings" from Conrad Aiken, and that Costa has made too much of the Jungian organon in interpreting Lowry's use of myth and symbol.

Allen, Walter. "The Masterpieces of the Forties," *On Contemporary Literature*. Ed. Richard Kostalanetz. New York: Avon Books, 1964, 419-21. As indicated earlier (see Review section of this Note), Allen considers *Under the Volcano* the finest novel written by an Englishman during the 1940s. The mild qualification in Allen's praise should not deter the reader from examining a very forthright, professional opinion by the author of *Writers on Writing*.

Barnes, Jim. "The Myth of Sisyphus in *Under the Volcano*," *Prairie Schooner*, Winter, 1968, 341-48. Some critic had to come up with an application of Camus' The *Myth of Sisyphus* to *Under the Volcano*. Barnes is fairly convincing in fitting the Lowry novel into the absurdist tradition.

Bradbrook, M. C. *Literature in Action: Studies in Continental & Commonwealth Society*. New York: Barnes & Noble, Inc., 1972. Chap. 6 ("Canada from Sea to Sea; the Single Image"). The most convincing argument for "anointing" Lowry as not only a Canadian writer, but by far the best of all Canadian writers.

Burgess, Anthony. "Europe's Day of the Dead," *Spectator* (1/20/67), 74. Take a bit of the Prometheus myth, add a dash of T. S. Eliot's "J. Alfred Prufrock" (see "traces" of some of the language of that poem in the novel), and you have another characterization of the Consul.

Corrigan, Matthew. "Malcolm Lowry, New York Publishing, & the 'New Illiteracy,'" *Encounter* XXXV, 1 (July, 1970), 88-83. This is a "second thought" on Corrigan's part, after having overpraised the publisher two years earlier for having put out an ineptly stitched-together version of *Dark As the Grave Wherein My Friend Is Laid* as a "finished" novel.

(See other Corrigan entry below in "Other Works" section.) This critic's position is both vacillating and ambiguous. One other possible explanation for his position is that in his more compassionate moments he is trying to overcompensate for the "illiteracy" of the twelve publishers who rejected the penultimate version of *Under the Volcano*.

Costa, Richard H. "Lowry/Aiken Symbiosis," *The Nation* (6/26/67), 823-26. A very readable effort to trace the transition from Conrad Aiken's character Hambo (in *Ushant*) to Lowry's Consul. The article was later incorporated into Costa's full-length study of Lowry.

Day, Douglas. "Of Tragic Joy," *Prairie Schooner*, Winter, 1963, 354-62. Lowry as a humorous writer - if one can agree to substitute the Consul's tequila and mescal for Falstaff's sack.

Dodson, Daniel B. *Malcolm Lowry*. New York: Columbia University Press, 1970 (in Columbia Essays on Modern Writers, Ed. W. Y. Tindall). Dodson applies a strictly modern critical yardstick to *Under the Volcano* and finds it to be a flawed but genuine masterpiece.

Doyen, Victor. "Elements Toward a Spatial Reading of Malcolm Lowry's *Under the Volcano*," *English Studies* 50 (1968), 65-74. A comparison with Joyce's *Ulysses* leads this critic to conclude that Lowry's novel is also unlinear in structure and should therefore be read as an extended piece of poetic prose. By so doing, the reader will eventually find most of the fragments, allusions, digressions, and fanciful interludes falling into place. In the light of so many of modern literature's formless and amorphous novels, the suggestion is somewhat gratuitous. *Under the Volcano* may not be a non-novel or an anti-novel, but it is certainly a novel. (Compare, for example, Nabokov's and Pynchon's novels as just a few examples that Lowry anticipated.)

Edmonds, Dale. "*Under the Volcano*: A Reading of the 'Immediate Level,'" *Tulane Studies in English*, XVI (1968), 63-105. If we can accept "the level of people, places, events and circumstances within a fictional world that much resembles our own," Edmonds suggests, then *Under the Volcano* "communicates most effectively." Since Lowry did not make a conscious effort to establish his novel as that contemporaneous, the premise is interesting if not wholly acceptable.

Gass, William H. *Fiction and the Figures of Life.* New York: Alfred A. Knopf, 1970, pp. 55–76 ("In Terms of the Toenail: Fiction and the Figures of Life"). What is most refreshing to Gass is that Lowry (unlike some of the more traditional, objective novelists) never attempted to establish any kind of distance between himself and the characters and situations in his books. This, Gass finds, is especially true of *Under the Volcano*.

Hicks, Granville. "One Great Statement," *Saturday Review* (12/4/65), 39–40. A Johnny-come-lately, albeit favorable, critic of *Under the Volcano*. He likes the second, hardbound American edition of the novel (he apparently hadn't read the first or 1947 edition), perhaps because of his unstinting admiration for Lowry's own defense of the novel in the Jonathan Cape letter of 1946 (which became available to the general reader in the *Selected Letters* in 1965).

Hirschman, Jack. "Kabbala/Lowry, etc." *Prairie Schooner*, Winter, 1963, 347–53. Taking off from the few references to the Cabbala in *Under the Volcano* (including Hugh's cursory examination of the several books on magic and mysticism in the Consul's library), Hirschman concludes that for Lowry elaborate symbolism, such as in the Cabbala, must be accepted as more than a mere literary device; it can be of enormous help to the reader in comprehending the several levels of meaning on which Lowry's frequently metaphorical prose was operating. The thesis is more elaborately developed in Perle Epstein's full-length study of *Under the Volcano*."

Kilgallin, Anthony R. "*Faust* and *Under the Volcano*," *Canadian Literature* No. 26 (Autumn, 1965), 43–54. For this critic, there is more Faust than Adam in the Consul.

Markson, David. "Myth in *Under the Volcano*," *Prairie Schooner*, Winter, 1963, 339–46. For this friend and critic, there is more Odysseus than Faust or Adam in the Consul.

McCormick, John. *Catastrophe and Imagination: A Reinterpretation of the Recent English and American Novel*. London and New York: Longmans Green & Co., 1957, pp. 85–89. In examining the causes of the **catastrophe** in *Under the Volcano*, the writer concludes that Lowry was concerned mainly with "the nature of love in a fragmented society." No se puede vivir sin amar, obviously.

New, W. H. *Articulating West: Essays on Purpose and Form in Modern Canadian Literature*. Toronto: New Press, 1972, pp. 189–205. New joins Hirschman and Epstein in asserting that Lowry was a conscious, unabashed Cabbalist.

Shorter, Kingsley. "Lowry's Private Trip," The *New Leader* (9/15/69), 14–16. Shorter dissents from the Lowry-as-Cabbalist school. "Magnificent as the book is,... *Under the Volcano* remains a very private trip." Was Shorter insisting that since Lowry took no trip-inducing drugs (and we have no evidence that he did), there was no need for **metaphysical** reinforcement of Lowry's apparently chronic sense of doom? Perhaps; but take away the special flavor provided in the novel by occultism, mysticism, Cabbalism, and the like, and one finds that the novel has lost that rare quality of strangeness and unreality that one associates with life at the high altitudes of Mexico.

Spender, Stephen. *Introduction, Under the Volcano*. Philadelphia: Lippincott, 1965, pp. vii-xxvi. Next to Lowry's own 1946 letter to Jonathan Cape (which Spender had not read earlier), this essay is by far the best introduction to the novel. Spender not only applies the acumen and insights of a poet to the Lowry novel; he also clearly delineates the extensive debt the structure of the novel owes to cinematic techniques.

Tindall, W. Y. "Many-Leveled Fiction: Virginia Woolf to Ross Lockridge." *College English*, X, 2 (November, 1948), 68–69. Note the date of this article, just one year after publication of *Under the Volcano* itself! In addition to the generally favorable and intensive evaluation of the novel, Tindall recognized the similarities between Lowry's and Woolf's handling of the interior monologue.

Toynbee, Philip. "Another Season in Hell," *The Observer* (4/29/62) 26. Toynbee recognizes many of the affinities Lowry had with Rimbaud and Baudelaire, and with other French Symbolists. For him, *Under the Volcano* is "one of the great English novels of this century."

Tuohy, Frank. "Day of a Dead Man," *Spectator* (8/27/61). The novel is a highly flawed work (not so original an observation), but "*Under the Volcano* is one of the great English novels of this century."

Wain, John. "Another Room in Hell," *The Atlantic Monthly*, CCXXII (August, 1968), 84–86. As is to be expected of one of England's "Angry Young Men," Wain takes strong exception to the self-centeredness Lowry is guilty of in *Under the Volcano*.

Widmer, Eleanor. "The Drunken Wheel: Malcolm Lowry and *Under the Volcano*," *The Forties: Fiction, Poetry, Drama*, ed. Warren French, Deland (Fla.): Everrett/Edwards, 1968, 217–26. Widmer conceives of *Under the Volcano* as a kind of patchwork quilt (cf. Aiken's similar evaluation). Too often, she says, the novel fails to come down to earth to recognize the natural possibilities for **irony**, chance, coincidence, and other natural, human forces.

Woodburn, John. "Dazzling Disintegration," *Saturday Review of Literature* (2/22/47), 9–10. We have already quoted from this article in the section entitled Reviews. However, it is worth repeating part of the statement again, bearing in mind that this review was one of the first to come upon publication of the first edition of *Under the Volcano*. It required no second reading of the novel to convince Woodburn that *Under the Volcano* is "a work of genius."

Woodcock, George. "Under Seymour Mountain," *Canadian Literature* No. 8, Spring, 1961, 3-6. Woodcock believes that Lowry may validly be placed alongside Proust both in technique and in all-embracing literary objective.

Wright, Terence. "*Under the Volcano*: The Static Art of Malcolm Lowry," *Ariel*, I, 4 (October, 1970), 67-76. A much-needed observation (or at least a summary) of the many-faceted techniques employed by Lowry: poetry, music, film, architecture, etc.

OTHER WORKS

Benham, David. "Lowry's Purgatory: Versions of 'Lunar Caustic,'" *Canadian Literature* No. 44 (Spring, 1970), 28-37. How Lowry converted his stay in Bellevue Hospital (1935) into a novella. Clinical observation of the D. T.'s was also incorporated into *Under the Volcano*.

Corrigan, Matthew. "Masks and the Man: The Writer As Actor," *Shenandoah*, XIX (Summer, 1968), 89-93. An extremely favorable criticism (later recanted) of the efforts of Douglas Day and Margerie Bonner Lowry to "prepare" the unfinished version of *Dark As the Grave Wherein My Friend Is Laid* for publication. Despite some reservations about the book as a novel, Corrigan had nothing but praise for the way in which the book reveals Lowry as a man of many personae.

Durrant, Geoffrey. "Death in Life: Neo-Platonic Elements in 'Through the Panama,'" *Canadian Literature* No. 44 (Spring, 1970), 13-27. How and why Lowry used excerpts from Coleridge's Ancient Mariner as marginal glosses. The use of Platonic elements (i.e., the significance of compass or regional directions, as explained earlier in this Note) is conventional.

Tiessen, Paul G. "Malcolm Lowry and the Cinema," *Canadian Literature* No. 44 (Spring, 1970), 38-49. The film, says the critic, is more than a source of method for Lowry; it is also "a **metaphor** to express the tormented, surrealistic world of his characters." This is a valuable contribution, and also a much-needed extension of the remarks made by Spender (in his Introduction to the 1965 edition of *Under the Volcano*) on Lowry's use of the cinema.

Woodcock, George, ed. *Malcolm Lowry: The Man and His Work*. Vancouver: University of British Columbia Press, 1971. This compendium of many of the critical articles on Lowry that appeared in *Canadian Literature* over a period of ten years (many of these articles may be found in this bibliography) is more than a festschrift. Lowry's many shortcomings, as well as his many virtues, are covered in this "casebook." Woodcock is to be commended for not going completely overboard in praise of Canada's most famous adopted (literary) "native son." He's there - warts (and quarts) and all.

www.ingramcontent.com/pod-product-compliance
Lightning Source LLC
LaVergne TN
LVHW011708060526
838200LV00051B/2802